W. W. GOODPASTURE, EDITOR

when not) to fertilize, what colors are available in various flowers. Mr. Carleton suggests bulb flowers for diverse uses — in formal gardens, rockeries, fields, shady corners. He has also

(see back end paper)

Hardy Bulbs

Rinehart's Garden Library

W. W. GOODPASTURE, GENERAL EDITOR

Already Published:

Evergreens	*L. L. Kumlien*
Small Fruits	*Ralph E. Barker*
Vegetables	*Jack M. Swartout*
Annuals	*Ann Roe Robbins*
Roses	*Roy E. Shepherd*
Lawns	*John D. Bernard*
Perennials	*Marjorie P. Johnson*
Hardy Bulbs	*R. Milton Carleton*

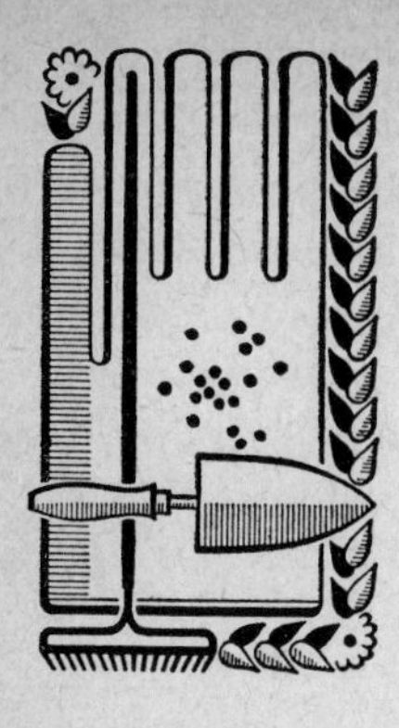

HARDY BULBS

R. Milton Carleton

illustrated by Rebecca and Douglas Merrilees

Rinehart & Company, Inc.

232 Madison Ave.

New York 16, N. Y.

103 St. Clair Ave., West

Toronto 5, Canada

Published simultaneously in Canada
by Clarke, Irwin & Company, Ltd., Toronto

Printed in the United States of America

Library of Congress Catalog Card Number: 55–5083

Contents

I.	HARDY BULBS	9
II.	GENERAL CULTURE	19
III.	CULTURE	39
IV.	DAFFODILS, NARCISSI AND JONQUILS	45
V.	HYACINTHS	53
VI.	THE MINOR BULBS	55
VII.	LILIES	66
VIII.	IRISES	78

GUIDE TO FLOWERS SHOWN ON COVER

1. *Tulip*
2. *Japanese Iris*
3. *Narcissus*
4. *Hyacinth*
5. *Iris*
6. *Daffodil*
7. *Lily*
8. *Parrot Tulip*

chapter one

Hardy bulbs

If there are any professional horticulturists in the audience, let them look the other way. I am not going to attempt to write *the* definitive work on bulbs, complete to the last genus and species. Instead, I want to introduce the beginner to an amazingly rich group of plants which includes some of the world's loveliest flowers.

The new gardener is apt to classify all brownish clumps of vegetable matter as bulbs if they grow underground and produce flowers. To him it means little that a gladiolus grows from a corm instead of a true bulb, that an iris produces a rhizome, or that the begonias he plants are tuberous instead of bulbous.

Dealers in bulbs make no more of an effort to be scientific. They unblushingly offer 100 BEAUTIFUL GLADIOLUS BULBS FOR $4.00 on the same counter as 12 GLAMOROUS TUBEROUS BEGONIA BULBS FOR $2.98. All this inaccuracy, distasteful as it may be to the botanist, hurts no one, so long as we are satisfied with what we buy when it flowers.

Bulbs important in the garden

What does matter is that the gardener understand how important these bits of inert brown vegetable matter can be in his garden. As unimpressive as they may seem before they are planted, no other group of plants will reward him as richly for so little effort. Equally important, he will find that bulbs are easy to grow, flowering in spite of the errors he is bound to make when planting them for the first time. No class of plant material, unless it be seeds, possesses such tremendous vitality.

This urge to grow arises from the fact that a bulb is a device developed by plants to carry them through periods during the year which are unfavorable for growth. In many bulbs, next year's plant is already formed, even to the flower bud which may have to wait eight to ten months before it can begin to expand. Some will actually flower on a window sill without soil or water, so eager are they to complete their life cycle.

The idea of a bulb as a device for overcoming adverse conditions should be understood. Only when we fully appreciate the purpose behind a bulb can we realize why it fits so well into those artificial plots for growing plants that we call gardens. Because it stores food and energy enough to crowd an entire year's growth into a few short weeks of life above ground, a bulb can use garden space for a period of time too short for other plants to complete the cycle from seed to flower. The most important use of bulbs, therefore, is to fill such gaps in the garden year.

Adapted to shade

A good example of where bulbs can fit in such gaps is found in the yard where the soil is shaded by trees and shrubs from late spring until fall. Along the north side of a hedge in particular, there will be areas which are reached by sunshine only in spring. As the trees and shrubs leaf out, these areas are cut off from the sun, so that only plants which tolerate deep shade will survive during the summer.

During this brief moment in the sun, spring-flowering bulbs have their day. Drawing upon nourishment stored underground the spring before, they burst through the soil, form leaves and produce flowers in a few short weeks. Before the trees and shrubs can again shut off the sun, they have manufactured and stored enough food for next spring's brief burst of life. Inside the bulb will be laid down the leaves and flowers which will appear the next spring.

The fact that snow does not melt until late on the north side of a hedge does not seem to matter at all. Often this is an advantage, keeping too-eager shoots from being nipped by late frosts.

In perennial borders

Bulbs are not limited to shady areas. Hardy bulbs are equally at home in other parts of the garden. The perennial border, usually at its best in early summer, has little to offer during the months of spring. Since many bulbs produce their flowers and are out of the way before the time the perennial border opens its big show, they are perfect plant material to fill in the garden picture. For at least three months in spring, they should form the basis of the perennial border. Starting with the earliest snowdrops, which open while traces of snow still linger in the shadows, bulbs will produce a continuous procession of color until the last late tulips fade just before the peonies and Oriental poppies appear.

In the lawn

I have a natural hesitation in recommending the planting of bulbs in the lawn. This is not an easy thing to do well, and I mention it only because the idea holds such fascination for beginning gardeners. They see a lawn bright with crocuses and daffodils, and immediately they must have the same. Certainly there is no more exciting way to use these early spring flowers, out in the open where they contrast so vividly with the new green of young grass.

Although not easy to do, naturalizing bulbs in the grass is possible. With attention to culture, they can be grown in this way so they will return year after year and flower freely.

Rock gardens

Thank heavens, the fad for rock gardens has run its course. You don't have to be too old to remember the time when every house in a city block would have its pile of stones, with anemic marigolds and geraniums sprouting from every crevice.

This fad is over, and good riddance to bad rubbish, too. This does not mean that I hate rock gardens. On the contrary, I hail the passing of rock-garden puddings because I love the right kind. There is no more attractive spot in the world than a really good planting among rocks where plants seem to be a living part of the stratum on which they grow. Obviously, such gardens do not belong out on the level prairie where they must be built up artificially.

Where rockeries really belong—in areas where obtrusive rocks and ledges make cultivated borders difficult—there is nothing lovelier in spring than masses of bulbs flowering in natural groups among the green-gray foliage of alpine plants. Here is one place where species or botanical tulips are at home.

There are the wild forms that come from climates so different from ours that we cannot easily meet their cultural needs. These are not happy in the open border. Instead, they prefer pockets among the stones where they can soak up summer heat, and where they can enjoy the sharp drainage most of them need to survive. Rockeries are fine, too, for the smaller bulbs (minor, as some people call them). Here scillas, snowdrops, species crocuses and similar gems which are hard to place in more formal settings, seem perfectly at home.

Woods, fields and corners

Not all of us must limit our gardening to the small lots on which most modern houses are built. The housewife on the farm, for instance, who must crowd as much gardening as possible into a busy life, finds bulbs particularly rewarding. They can spill over the fence across the back "forty" and into the wood lot, where they will thrive and multiply without special care.

An adventure for the city farmer is to plant a hayfield with narcissi. These are not expensive and a planting of a few thousand bulbs will make a wonderful show even the first year. If the hay is not cut until midsummer, the bulbs will have time to ripen, and will return with increased beauty every spring.

Even in towns and villages, there are often open spaces which cry for bulbs planted in masses and drifts. One friend of mine, starting with a few hundred bulbs thirty years ago, has extended his planting on two acres of woods until he now has over two million narcissi that carpet the floor of a small forest with yellow every spring.

On smaller grounds, there are always difficult corners that cry for some treatment. If they get as much as four hours of sun a day during the growing season, they ought to be planted to bulbs. The fact that weeds may later take over such corners, or even smother a field in summer does not prevent their use. By the time weeds begin to compete for sun, water and food, most bulbs have completed their growth and disappeared for the year.

Formal beds

Formal bedding reached its greatest development during Queen Victoria's time, then went into a slow decline. This laborious, time-consuming way of gardening was not suited to the pace of modern life and for several decades has been nearly dead.

Oddly enough, the modern ranch house, the perfect antithesis of the Victorian home, is responsible for a revival of interest

1. Formal planting of tulips along driveway and under picture window

in formal bedding. Florists everywhere report a manifold increase in demand for geraniums, lantanas and other plants of Victorian days.

The reason for this revival is the need for a special type of planting on the small lots of modern houses. Here is an architectural style that presents a real problem to the old-time landscaper, whose stock in trade was "foundation" planting. Here is a house that has no foundation to plant. Lots are too small to justify an axis or "point of interest" planting. About the only chance for using ornamental plants is against the base of the walls, under picture windows or along walks and drives. Here, formal plantings are almost the only treatment that can be given.

No plant is better adapted to the rigid demands of formal bedding than the hyacinth (where purse and climate permit) or

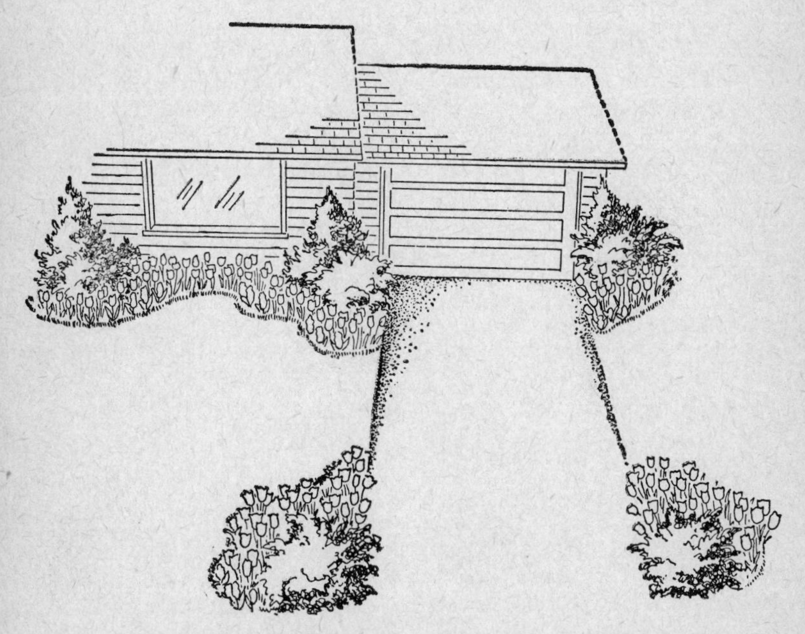

2. *Informal planting under window and at corners*

single and double tulips. Stiff, formal ribbons of Early Double Tulips along the walk go with the modern ranch house like ham goes with eggs. Owners of this type of house find that such formal ribbons are logically the first planting done if they move in during late summer or early fall.

Over these, annuals like petunias, seeds of which will survive over winter, are often seeded for bloom when the tulips fade.

The long season garden

There is nothing new about planting a garden that will flower from early spring until killing frost. Most attempts at laying out such a garden, however, fall short of success. The weakness of most of these is that they don't solve the fact that few plants can flower well for more than two months at a stretch.

My favorite layout for such a garden calls for the use of minor bulbs, daffodils, tulips and other bulbs, over which are seeded late in fall certain annuals whose seeds can survive freezing. These annuals sprout early in spring, usually flowering as the last tulips fade. They are not long-lived, since most of them are cool-weather species like poppies, larkspur, etc., and are past their prime by early July.

About the time these annuals begin to sprout, other species more tolerant of warm weather are seeded in cold frames, where they can be held until needed. These are moved in to produce the third wave of bloom. In the meantime, hardy chrysanthemums are being grown in six-inch pots, ready to move in when their buds are first showing color.

Such a schedule sounds too ambitious for the amateur's first year, unless he wants to go to the expense of buying the bedding annuals and the hardy chrysanthemums. Once he has gained some experience, however, the skill needed is not too great for the average home owner. Two or three cold frames, occupying a few square feet of space at the back of the lot should be ample to grow all the plants needed. Because the bedding plants are started late, no artificial heat is needed. The chrysanthemums can be grown in rows in the vegetable garden.

Bulbs for cutting

No home ever has too many cut flowers. The bulbs needed to supply these in early spring can often be salvaged from regular plantings without having to buy them. A row of "splits" or "slabs"—side bulbs removed from the main bulb before it is planted—will provide plenty of narcissi planting stock. Undersized tulips, if planted in a row in the vegetable garden and not fertilized, will gradually grow to flowering size. Hyacinths that have been forced can be planted out and in a couple of years should produce some long loose spikes which are lovely in arrangements.

Summer and fall bulbs

So far we have considered only the bulbs that flower in spring. Not all hardy bulbs produce their bloom in a single burst of glory early in the growing season. If as a matter of convenience we consider the tall, bearded irises among the bulbs (to place them near their bulbous relatives), it is obvious that some of the best of the summer's flowers can also be grown in this way.

The lilies are an excellent example of these summer bulbs. Here is a group of plants so lovely in its many varieties that hobby gardeners often use them to plant entire gardens. The lily is the only flower that challenges the rose in popular interest. In a recent survey, investigators found that next to the rose, more people could identify the lily than any other flower.

A little-known but fascinating summer-flowering bulb is the hardy amaryllis. In spring, it produces exotic straplike leaves that grow for a few weeks, then die down and disappear completely. Magically, in late summer, green spears suddenly shoot out of the ground, reaching full height in two or three days. From these appear several clear lilac-colored trumpets about four inches long. These last for about a week, then fade and pass out as mysteriously as they did in spring, only to rise again the next year gaining strength for another burst of bloom in fall.

Bulbs essential

Because they fit so beautifully into gaps in the garden year, bulbs serve a purpose which cannot be met with any other class of plant material. The proper use of bulbs is the mark of a good gardener. Without them, the job of keeping the garden full of color in spring would be almost impossible. Thanks to the marvelous list of bulbous material available in commerce today, even the beginner has a chance to give his garden a professional "finish."

chapter two

General culture

There is danger in reasoning from experience with one type of bulb to include all that grow from underground structures of this kind. They differ so much that no general instruction can be given that applies to all of them. At the same time, there are certain fundamentals which are common to all forms, and which can be covered in a general discussion of their needs.

Soils

Many writers prate glibly about the need for growing bulbs in "rich" soil. While some are careful to state that fresh manures are bad for bulbs, just as many are insistent that only organic fertilizers are safe to use on them.

Who is right? Before that question can be answered, perhaps we ought to go back to fundamentals, study the plant in its native home and then work out a culture based on its needs. As we do so, however, we must keep in mind that this idea of duplicating a natural habitat can be carried too far.

A garden is essentially an artificial place to grow plants. Your climate may be nothing like that of a bulb's native home. The day may be of a different length (highly important with some plants); you may have more rainfall or less; temperatures may differ widely and so on.

At the same time, we know that a water lily cannot grow in the desert, nor will a cactus grow with wet feet. We ought to be intelligent enough to draw a few general conclusions from our knowledge of where a plant came from.

Poor soils for bulbs

Remember what I said about a bulb being a device for overcoming adverse conditions? With the possible exception of the lily, bulbs discussed in this book are found growing in the wild where soils are relatively poor. Many of them grow on sandy loams or in gravelly soils. These soils do not retain plant foods well, even though rotting leaves and other vegetable matter on top of them allow such plant foods to seep in.

Anyone looking at the near-arid sandy soils in Asia Minor, on which tulips originated, will wonder how the bulbs survive at all. Here the spring rains start up growth but summer drought permits only semiarid plants to remain in active growth at that time. Because of a location at quite a high elevation, the native home of the tulip is not too hot in summer. Chilly nights at this altitude keep soil temperatures lower than they would be in the Middle West, closer perhaps to those found in New England.

High fertility stops flowering

The tulip has evolved to survive under these conditions. Its roots forage for food in relatively poor soil, storing enough in the bulb during the brief growing season to carry the plant for an entire year. If, for some reason, food in excess of the small needs of the bulb does occur, the bulb responds to this stimulus by splitting.

The mother bulb, weakened by this splitting, usually stops flowering. Often it never again forms a flower bud. Soon a small colony forms around the mother bulb, all members of which compete for the food available.

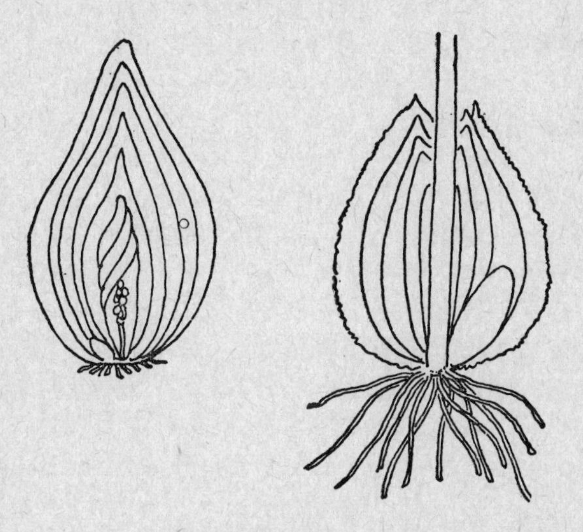

3. *Splitting. This formation of small bulbs inside the mother bulb is caused by excess of food and will result in cessation of flowering*

With all this competition for food, those which cannot flower on limited nourishment will gradually be eliminated, since they will produce no seed to carry the race beyond the area occupied by the single colony.

To a lesser degree, this same process takes place in narcissi, which, however, can survive richer living than can tulips.

This splitting tendency is important to the home gardener because once it takes place the new division needs two to three years before it can accumulate enough reserve food to flower.

Overfeeding in an attempt to stimulate flowering won't help because this simply causes the new bulb to split sooner.

Often we hear the gardener complain, "My tulips don't last any time at all. The first year or two they are nice, then all I get are a lot of leaves and no flowers." What has happened is obvious. His bulbs have been planted in rich soil and have followed their natural tendencies. Since the excess food of the mother bulb is used in producing the new "split," no flower bud is laid down. In his anxiety to force bloom, the gardener then pours on fertilizer. This produces more division until the entire planting is throwing up only a single leaf to each bulb, indicating that the new bulbs are not large enough to bloom.

Lean rations

The answer here is to put tulips (and to some extent other bulbs) on a diet. When, however, we put humans on a diet, we don't shut off all food: we merely regulate the intake, but make sure that the food we do supply is complete in all the elements of nutrition.

Here is our clue to feeding bulbs. They cannot be grown in sterile sand or on other soils devoid of all food. What they require is a reasonably good garden soil in which other plants are grown during the summer with enough fertilizer for the use of these summer occupants. What is left over when these plants are through growing—roots, dead bacteria, remnants of organic matter that decayed too late to be used by annuals, and even remnants of fertilizer—should provide all the food tulips will require.

Not for specimen blooms

What fooled us in the past is that gardeners were always trying to grow specimen blooms. Intrigued by the spectacular specimens on the great Keukenhoff Estate in Holland (the "showcase" of the Dutch bulb industry) or the magnificent individual blooms in European flower shows, many American specialists have asked for directions for growing these. Out of these instructions, I suspect, have come many of the direction sheets issued by dealers.

One thing is wrong with all this. We *can* grow exhibition flowers in our back yards, but only if we want to pay the price. This calls for using the bulbs one year and then discarding them. By forced feeding when the shoots are just emerging from the soil, we can increase the length of petals on tulips as much as ½ inch to 1 inch. They will make a magnificent show, but the bulbs will be worth very little afterward.

Such overfed bulbs may even produce a flower the second year, but the third year will usually see them on the way out. This, incidentally, is one reason why the idea of lifting bulbs every two years sometimes works well in practice: the digging prevents too great an accumulation of food and saves the bulb.

The gardener who can afford to replace his tulips every two years can ignore the cautions I have given and feed liberally. The result will be a splendid show for, at the most, two years.

Most of us, however, cannot afford this luxury, but must try to make our bulbs last as long as possible. Hence the wisdom of keeping their diet on the lean side. Since we want to use tulips as masses of color, and not as individual specimens, the fact that they may be half an inch or so short of maximum size should make very little difference.

On poor soils

Not all of us, however, have good garden soil. Many of us must garden on poor sand, on soils high in gravel or on land that has been farmed for generations and is worn out. Elsewhere, erosion has stripped away topsoil, leaving only the infertile subsoil exposed.

On such soils, bulbs must be fed. The time of feeding is important. Fertilizers are best applied in early spring, just as the shoot is breaking through the ground, and before the leaf itself unfurls. This fertilizer should be a mineral fertilizer (sometimes called chemical plant food) and not an organic material. Contrary to common impression, organic fertilizers can be definitely harmful. Work at the Department of Agriculture on bulbs shows that they have far more disease when their food is from organic sources than when mineral fertilizers are used.

In my own work, I find that the tulip disease known as "tulip fire" (caused by a fungus the plant picks up as it breaks through the surface) is fostered by a layer of organic matter on the surface.

About a pound of good mixed general fertilizer should feed the bulbs on an area five by ten feet (50 square feet). If more than this is applied, even on poor soils, the danger of stimulating splitting is greatly increased.

Complete fertilizer essential

It is important that this fertilizer be complete, that is, it should contain potash and phosphorus as well as nitrogen. If possible, it should also contain the minor or trace elements, some of which are very important in growing bulbs. Research at the United States Department of Agriculture showed that when potash and phosphorus were included in fertilizer mixtures, they had a tendency to reduce the danger of disease; results were not as satisfactory when nitrogen was used alone.

This is a good place to drag that old panacea of the English gardener—bone meal—into the cold light of day. Any book on gardening written over five years ago probably copied verbatim the recommendation made by some old British work, advocating the liberal use of bone meal on bulbs. It is said to be the best of all fertilizers for this class of plant material.

Probably it is, if the bulbs are planted on good soil. But the reason it is good here is that it is no good. That is, it does nothing, and therefore does no harm. It can be used, *ad nauseam*, without affecting growth. The reason is quite simple: on most American soils, bone meal is quickly locked up into insoluble form, which is of practically no use to bulbs.

It is not uncommon, when working with other plants, to find that they can be stimulated into greater growth by the addition of soluble forms of phosphorus, even though bone meal has been added yearly for decades. The only plant-food element of any consequence in bone meal *is* phosphorus, but from this source it is not readily available to plants.

Bone meal performs a useful function because it gives the gardener something to do. He feels that he must apply a fertilizer, so throwing some of this white powder (which does have a convincing smell) onto the soil satisfies him. Since it does no harm, everyone is happy. Personally, I prefer to eliminate the bone meal and use the money to buy more bulbs.

Depth of planting

Although depth of planting is covered in chart form elsewhere, it should also be considered in relation to splitting. True, if bulbs are set 10 inches deep (provided the soil is not heavy clay loam or clay), they will survive better without splitting than at a shallower depth in rich soil.

The effect is one of compelling the plant to use up more of its reserve food to break through the ground before it can replace its supply. When tulips are grown as groups in the perennial border, on soil that is naturally rich, this trick is worth while.

If it can be done, however, I find it much easier to avoid rich soil and to plant at normal depth.

Mulches

Quite often instructions for planting all bulbs call for mulching them after planting. This is an excellent suggestion, provided the mulch is not one of manure, compost or other decayed or partially decayed organic matter. All bulbs are more or less sensitive to fungi (moldlike organisms in the soil) which live in organic matter. Tulip fire is often passed on to bulbs by such decayed matter. Suitable mulching materials are pine needles, marsh hay, clean wheat straw, cut Christmas tree branches, excelsior and vermiculite. These materials are clean and will not cause trouble.

Depth to plant

Except for deep planting already recommended to prevent tulips from splitting, the depth at which to plant various bulbs can be read from the following chart. This is not a fussy, measure-to-a-fraction-of-an-inch business. You can err ½ inch to 1 inch on the smaller bulbs and 2 inches to 3 inches on the large ones and they will still grow. The one exception is the Madonna lily, which is particular about the depth at which it is planted.

Sometimes the recommendation is made that bulbs be planted more shallowly in clay soils than in sands. What usually happens is that tulips are set at a depth of 4 inches, appear far too soon in spring and are badly injured by freezing.

If the soil is too heavy for bulbs to be planted at the depths recommended below, it should either be modified, or the bulbs not planted at all.

It is important to remember that all measurements are from soil level to the *top* of the bulb after it is planted, not the bottom. To determine the depth of the hole, add to these measurements the length from bulb tip to base.

Planting depths for bulbs

The depth refers to the amount of soil *above* the bulb. The hole or trench should be dug to the depth of covering soil plus the height of the bulb.

Chionodoxa	3 inches
Crocuses	2 inches
Daffodils and Narcissi	Twice as much dirt over them as the depth of the bulb. About 3 inches for small species, 6 or 7 inches for large.
Fritillaria	Crown Imperial 4 inches. Guinea Hen 3 inches.
Grape Hyacinths	3 inches
Hyacinths	3 inches in clay, 4 inches in loamy soil
Iris	½ inch soil over rhizomes. Bulbous iris—3 inches for miniatures like Iris *reticulata,* 5 inches for large bulbs.
Lilies	In general, stem-rooting lilies are planted 8 inches deep or 10 to 12 inches in loamy soil. Other lilies about 5 inches deep with the following exceptions: American Turkscap, 6 inches; Easter lily, 8 inches; Henry's Lily, 8 to 10 inches; Leopard Lily, 4 to 5 inches; *Lilium formosanum,* 8 inches; Madonna Lily, 1½ inches; Meadow Lily, 6 inches; Nankeen Lily, 1½ inches; Regal Lily, 8 inches; Siberian Martagon Lily, 5 inches; Speciosum Lily, 8 inches.

Scillas	3 inches
Spring Snowflake	4 inches
Star of Bethlehem	2 inches
Tulips	6 to 8 inches in the North; 10 to 12 inches in the South.

Tulips in the South

In the South, another factor enters the picture. If soil temperatures around the bulb (particularly tulips) go much above 85 degrees, the bud inside is likely to be killed or injured. Narcissi are not as much affected, and the tender types like Paper Whites not at all. The hardier narcissi should go an inch or two deeper than shown. Tulips can go as deep as 10 to 12 inches. This calls for a loose, well-drained soil. A ground cover like petunias seeded over the beds in summer helps keep down temperatures.

How to plant

Beware the dibble. This is a blunt instrument driven into loose soil to make a hole in which bulbs are planted. In the hands of a really expert gardener, it is not too bad, but the amateur usually either packs the soil too tightly, or he leaves a pocket under the bulb so it is "hung" with the base in air instead of soil. Too, it is hard to measure actual depth with a dibble, if indeed it can be driven deep enough for planting most bulbs.

I prefer a trowel. My favorite is a strong long-handled weapon known as a Sprowel, measuring over 12 inches long. I don't know whether this particular tool is still made, but a satisfactory substitute can be had by cutting off the handle of a narrow tiling spade so as to make it usable while kneeling to plant bulbs.

Where formal beds are to be planted, as along the walk of a ranch house, the best plan is to remove the earth entirely. Don't throw it onto the grass, as it will be hard to remove later. I prefer to either throw it into a wheelbarrow as I go along, or onto boards laid nearby.

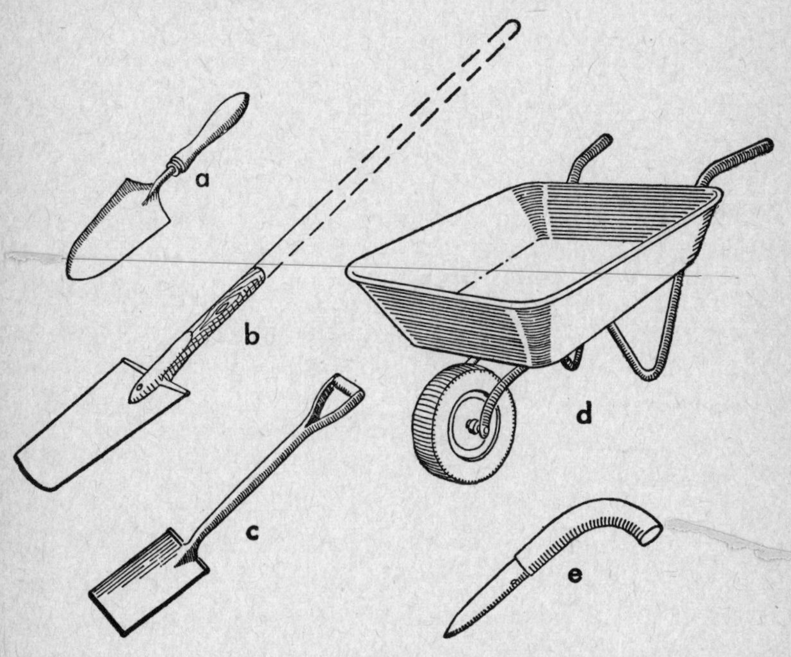

4. *Tools. a) Trowel. b) Sprowel. c) Spade. d) Wheelbarrow. e) Dibble (to be avoided by amateurs).*

The earth is removed to the depth recommended on the chart plus the depth of the bulb. Thus if the bulbs average 2 inches from base to tip, and the planting depth is 6 inches, dig out 8 inches of soil. Now set the bulbs with the proper spacing on the bottom of this excavation. Carefully dribble some of the dirt between the bulbs to hold them in place. Then fill in the rest of the soil.

You will find that, somehow, it has swelled in volume. Instead of the bulbs being covered to a depth of 6 inches, they may be 8 inches or more below the surface. Your next step is to take the hose and wet down the bed until it settles firmly. You won't be able to restore it to its original level, but don't worry about it: winter storms will settle the earth around the bulbs.

Uncovering

Where mulches are used, remember they are designed to keep beds frozen in spring as well as to keep frost out in fall until the bulbs can root. Leave them in place just so long as they help keep in frost and prevent early sprouting.

Once the shoots begin to break through under the mulch, however, it should be removed carefully. If this operation is delayed, the shoots will grow through it, and may be broken when removal is attempted. When the maple trees begin to flower, peek under the mulch to see if growth is beginning.

Tulips

Of all the blossoms of spring, none can match the tulip in beauty. Of the myriad flowers grown by man, it is one of the most artistic. Planted in bold masses, it becomes pure concentrated color unmatched in its season. The purity of a white Darwin, like Glacier, is unsurpassed. Only one flower, the viola, Black Imp, can match the depth of color exhibited by La Tulipe Noire. Between these two extremes can be found every tint and hue of the spectrum except pure blue. The tulip is one of the few flowers in existence which includes in its range yellows, near-blues, reds, purples and other solid colors along with such exotic variations as coffee brown and orange, salmon, rose and amber, violet with yellow, and so on.

Without equal in its season for color, the tulip also excels in beauty of line. Grow it against a dark yew hedge or out where its willowy stems can be seen against a blue sky.

For all its beauty, it is one of the sturdiest of bulbs. If grown with attention to its requirements, it can survive for years in the mixed border without any attention whatever, living off the crumbs left by the herbaceous plants. Actually, it thrives on neglect and is weakened by too-rich living, as we have already seen. When used for bedding in parks and cemeteries, I have seen the bulbs dug up soon after flowering and planted in an inconspicuous corner to ripen. Even with this rough treatment, I have been able to identify varieties in the planting which have not been in commerce for fifteen to twenty years.

One of the oldest plantings of tulips to come to my attention was on the estate of the late Mrs. Walter Brewster. She was one of the country's leading connoisseurs of bulbs and knew how to care for them. She showed me a planting of a Darwin which had been dropped from Dutch catalogues during World War I. The original planting, set long before 1914, was still flowering in 1946.

Long season of bloom

Often the complaint is made that tulips have too short a blooming season. When I hear this, I am sure that the man who says it is not an experienced gardener. In nine cases out of ten, he is a man who is bewitched by the name Darwin, and who has planted nothing but tulips listed under that heading in the catalogue. As fine as the Darwins are, they bloom for a relatively short time, being even more uniform in this respect than the closely related Breeder and Cottage varieties.

By proper selection of types and varieties, even if the botanical or species tulips are omitted, it is possible to have them in flower for fully two months.

Many types

As already suggested, the beginner will do well to pass up the tricky species or botanical tulips unless he has a rock garden in the sun, where they do splendidly. They are best left to the hobby gardener who is willing to give them the special care they need.

There is, however, one important exception to this recommendation. The species *Tulipa fosteriana,* a wild tulip from Turkey, is surprisingly tough and does well in cultivation in the United States. It has been the parent of several fine garden hybrids, of which The Big Boss and Scarlet Emperor are readily available. These will bloom weeks before the taller Cottage and Breeder Tulips.

The individual flowers are so large that they seem almost grotesque. An 8-inch bud on a 12-inch stem may sound out of proportion. However, the amazingly brilliant color—like a neon sign laid on the ground—is so startling at this early season that one or the other of these varieties really should be included.

Single and double early tulips

Next in season are the Single Early and Double Early Tulips. These grow between 8 and 12 inches tall and because of their short stems are not easily snapped off by wind. They come closer to the tulips of two hundred to three hundred years ago than any others in commerce today. They were developed for one purpose—planting in solid masses in beds and formal patterns. For this purpose, they are marvelous. As individual blooms, the Early Doubles are heavy and clumsy, but when seen en masse, they form solid sheets of color, either pure white, clear rose, bright rose or rich scarlet.

One frequent use (which prejudiced some people against

them) was for planting graves in cemeteries. However, this makes them nonetheless valuable for growing in broad ribbons along walks, or wherever a mass of clean bold color can be used.

The Single Early sorts can also be used for such planting, but are perhaps at their best in the perennial border. I like to plant them in irregular groups of six to twelve bulbs among the perennials, where they supply color for weeks before the first tall late tulips flower, and nearly two months before the first peony buds unfold.

Triumphs

The Triumphs represent a relatively new group of tulips which unfortunately was just becoming known when World War II broke out. Because these were not in big demand, the thrifty Dutch only kept small foundation stocks of the best, and concentrated on other classes where more profit could be made after the war.

Only within the past three or four years have Triumphs come into their own. Today, several varieties in this class are among the leading forcing varieties for commercial use. They excel for this purpose because they are two weeks ahead of the Darwins, equal to them in color and size, and superior as cut flowers. In height they range between 20 and 25 inches.

These same qualities help the Triumphs excel in the garden. They bridge the gap between the early class and the tall late-flowering classes. Incidentally, my favorite of all tulips is the Triumph Elisabeth Evers, unsurpassed in the beauty of its rich rose and white flowers.

Tall late tulips

If I were following the catalogue classification, the next group should be the Darwins. However, I want to destroy an illusion which has prevented many a gardener from enjoying some of the world's best tulips. Somehow, the promotion which was given the Darwins was so effective that this class earned a reputation which it does not deserve. Today, many gardeners think only of Darwins when they think of tulips.

True, at one time these flowered slightly ahead of the Cottage and Breeder types, and for this reason were preferred.

Another reason for favoring them was that the Darwin was supposed to have clear bright colors in reds and pinks, where other classes were weak.

Actually, the distinctions between Darwins, Cottage and Breeders no longer are valid. The older Cottage varieties tend to be somewhat smaller and shorter than Darwins, but the newer ones may be larger and taller. Breeders are supposed to be dull and dark, yet brilliant orange-yellow varieties like Dillenberg and Cherbourgh outshine many of the darker colors in Darwins.

Don't be confused by class names, but realize that Cottage, Darwin and Breeder varieties can be mixed in any way that pleases you. So long as they are planted with regard for height and color, no other differences need be considered.

Late double tulips

These doubled varieties of Darwins and other late tulips grow on much taller stems than the Double Early varieties, and the flowers are much more closely packed with petals. I find them completely without grace. They look like baseballs on top of 24-inch stems.

About the only use I can see for them is in enormous beds around monumental buildings, if the colors available fit into the landscape architect's scheme. Otherwise, they are floral curiosities of little beauty.

New parrot varieties

Although some catalogues lump all the Parrot tulips together, this is a crime against the newer varieties. Anyone who has ever grown the old-fashioned Parrot sorts would quickly pass over this class, and thus miss some of the finest of all tulips available today.

The older varieties have soft limp stems so floppy that the buds are almost on the ground before they open. By the time the flower is supposed to be at its best, it is so covered with mud as to be worthless.

The new Parrot tulips are entirely different. They are "breaks" or mutants of the finer Darwin and Cottage varieties. The petals are twisted and curled in odd and unusual forms. They retain the basic coloration of the original variety from which they came, but to this are added tints and shades of the same, curiously intermingled with streaks of green. As peculiar as this sounds, the effect is lovely.

These are perhaps the most artistic of all tulips, really beautiful in arrangements and for floral decoration.

Lily flowered tulips

These are developments from the old-time, long-petaled Cottage varieties. The petals are extremely long and graceful. When fully matured, they sometimes reflex like a fully opened magnolia, exposing the base of the petals. Along with the new Parrot varieties, they are widely used for artistic floral arrangements.

Tulip oddities

In the historic days of hysterical tulip speculation in Holland, the most desirable were curiously striped, speckled and blotched varieties with names like Bizzares, Bybloems, etc. While these tulips are still in commerce, the beginner should be warned that we now know these curious effects are the result of disease. This "breaking," as it is called, can be artificially produced by inoculating any plain-colored tulip with two different strains of virus disease. All Bybloems and Bizzares are the result of natural infestion with these two viruses.

For this reason, such tulips do not belong in the average garden. Similar striped and blotched tulips may arise spontaneously among normally solid-colored tulips. If so, they should be dug out at once and destroyed by burning.

Varieties

Tulip varieties are far more stable than any other group of flowering material in existence. For example, there is a Breeder Tulip called Bacchus which has been in commerce for over three hundred years and is still among the top varieties in its class.

During both World War I and World War II the Dutch were forced to reduce their list of varieties, and did so by throwing away most of the older sorts, keeping mostly the newer, more expensive kinds. For a year or two after each war was over, old familiar varieties were practically impossible to buy. The conservatism of tulip buyers, however, brought most of the old-timers back after a few years.

For this reason a list of tulip varieties is not likely to go out of date very fast. The following recommendations include some of the newer, better sorts as well as the best of the old favorites.

Species

Red Emperor, Scarlet Emperor, The Big Boss (all vivid neon red).

Single early

Couleur Cardinal (cardinal red); General De Wet (golden orange, with heavenly fragrance); Keiserkroon (bright scarlet edged yellow, centuries old, but still fine); Pink Beauty (bright rose pink); White Hawk (best white); Thomas Moore (apricot).

Double early

Murillo (rose pink); Schoonord (snowy white); Orange Nassau (red-orange); Vuurbaak (scarlet).

Triumph

Elisabeth Evers (rose pink over white, one of the finest of all tulips); Kansas (pure white); Ursa Minor (clear yellow, rather short, but magnificent color); Telescopium (violet-red); Crater (deep vermillion).

Cottage

Yellows: Golden Harvest, Mrs. John Scheepers, Moonlight, Mrs. Moon.
Brilliant Scarlet: Grenadier.
Rose, salmon and buff blends: Barbara Pratt, Dido, Marjorie Bowen.
White: Albion, Carrara.

Breeders

Bacchus (Concord grape purple); Cherbourg and Dillenberg (artistic gold-orange blends); Don Pedro (coffee brown); Louis XIV (regal purple and gold); Lucifer (orange).

Darwins

Reds: Bartigon, Charles Needham, City of Haarlem, Eclipse, Gloria Swanson, Utopia.

Pinks and rose: Afterglow, King George V, Princess Elizabeth (now the Queen); Pride of Zwannenberg, Prunus.

White: Glacier (the perfect white tulip).

Lavender and Purple: Faust, Greuze, Insurpassable, La Tulipe Noire, Queen of the Night.

Parrots

Blue Parrot, Violet Queen, Red Champion, Sunshine, Fantasy.

Lily flowered

Not generally available. Take what can be had.

chapter three

Culture

The general needs of bulbs have been covered in part in chapter two. Several other problems need to be considered, however,

One major argument among tulip fanciers is whether to dig the bulbs yearly, or to allow them to remain in the ground year after year. Even those who do not dig every fall often believe in lifting them every two or three years.

As the beginner will readily see, this means a lot of fussing. Not only does it call for labor in lifting and cleaning, but the danger of mixing up named varieties when out of the ground is considerable. Too, unless dry, cool storage (not too much over 70 degrees maximum, and not below 55 degrees minimum) can be provided, the flower buds can be hurt.

This matter of proper storage temperature is one which most people do not consider important. They believe bulbs can be stored in any shed or garage, even during summer heat.

Dutch specialists, however, consider storage temperature so important, even in their less torrid climate, that they build special structures to maintain proper readings.

True, temperatures in the 70's are not always possible to find in American basements and cellars. Sometimes a compromise is necessary, but this figure is certainly worth trying for.

In the South bulbs are often dug and put in cold storage for the summer. The most common error here is to use commercial storage space which is kept close to freezing. When readings below 50 degrees are used, changes take place inside the bulb which prepare it for immediate growth. When it is taken out of this low temperature and planted, it immediately begins to grow.

This can cause trouble in sections like Birmingham and Atlanta, where freezing temperatures occur after normal planting time. If, however, planting is delayed much past November, the bulbs can be hurt more by storage than by freezing. For this reason, clean mulches should be on hand to give some protection to the shoots as they emerge, should temperatures below 25° threaten. If frozen, the mulches delay thawing, reducing the damage done.

Leaving bulbs in

My preference, wherever it can be done, is for leaving bulbs in the ground year after year. If set deeply enough so they will be reasonably cool (approximately 6 to 8 inches in the North, 10 to 12 inches in the South) and a ground cover like petunias seeded over them, they will last for years. In the spring of 1953, I examined a planting of three thousand tulips I made in 1942. There were over two thousand of these still flowering. If they had been dug each year probably all three thousand would have "run out" by that time.

In warm soils

Often soil temperatures cannot be depended upon to remain low enough to keep tulips in good condition. Out on the Great

Plains, for example, summer temperatures go so high and remain there so long that the readings at 8 inches will go well above 80, the danger point.

With a ground cover and mulch, readings 8 inches down will approximate a level about 12 to 15 degrees below the daily average. Sooner or later, as heat accumulates in the soil, this margin narrows and the bulbs are hurt.

In such areas, if tulips are tried at all, the only answer is to dig and store as soon as the bulbs die down. If a cool root cellar is available, they are better off there than in the soil.

Heeling in

At times, bulbs must be dug up before the leaves start to turn yellow and die down. For example, when they are planted in the perennial border, they are in the way when the perennials must be reset. If allowed to remain until the border is dug in early fall, they are almost impossible to locate. Hence they must be dug when their foliage is still intact.

The best procedure is to lift them, leaving as much earth as

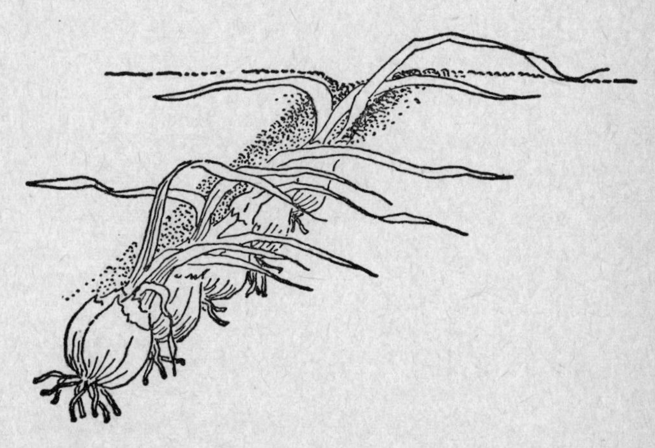

5. Heeling in bulb plants

possible clinging to them. Then replant them in an inconspicuous part of the garden until the foliage has died down. This replanting need not be very carefully done. Just throw enough earth over the bulbs to keep them moist until the foliage has withered. Such replanting is known as "heeling in."

Time to plant

When bulbs are left in the soil, one problem is automatically solved. When they are dug each year and replanted, they have a tendency to start growing earlier. If set out too early, sometimes they will send shoots above ground during mild spells in winter. Unless this growth is too long and temperatures drop sharply, the damage is usually limited to burned tips on the leaves when they unfold in spring. Sometimes, however, the flower buds are killed or injured and bloom is poor that year.

Bulbs planted at the recommended depths seldom start early when left in from year to year.

When new plantings are made, the ideal time to set out tulips is just after a sharp frost has killed annuals in the garden. Sometimes an unusual year comes along when annuals are in growth long past their normal season. The best guide in such a year is the leaves on elms and maples. Their falling is not entirely dependent upon frost; they will drop when a certain season is reached, regardless of weather. When the foliage of these trees is half fallen, plant tulips regardless of temperature; that is, plant them even if sharp frosts have not already occurred.

Late planting successful

When cold weather comes early and the ground freezes before its normal time, most beginning gardeners feel it is too late to plant tulips. On the contrary, I have pried off a frozen crust

2 to 3 inches thick between Christmas and New Year's Day, and planted both tulips and narcissi. The narcissi flowered rather short, but the tulips were normal in every way.

Oftentimes bulbs can be had at a bargain late in the season, particularly if freezes come early. I would beware of such offers from outlets that are not regular bulb dealers, such as chain stores and department stores. They never have proper storage facilities for bulbs, but keep them in rooms that are too warm. Usually the flower bud has been injured and no bloom can be expected the next spring.

Even when buying any quantity of bargain bulbs from regular seed stores late in the season, insist on the privilege of cutting a bulb or two. By cutting from the tip straight through the center of a bulb to the base, you will cut directly through the flower bud. Examine this carefully. If it shows brown stains, or if there are blackish streaks through it, that bulb is worthless.

If, however, the bud is either faint creamy white, or if the yellow stamens can be seen in the flower, the bulb is all right and would have grown normally.

Size of bulbs

If possible, try to buy out of original bags. If these are marked "Product of Holland," your chances are excellent, unless substitution has been made. This is not very likely. The Dutch Government sets up strict standards, and bulbs under flowering size are not allowed to be exported. Except for certain species tulips, and one or two Cottage varieties which never make big bulbs, all must exceed 11 centimeters in size. A bulb of this size will flower unless it is mishandled.

One of the curses of the industry is high-pressure advertisers who offer tulips at ridiculously low prices. Since the law now requires that the size be stated if a bulb is not of flowering size, watch for this item in the ads. Bulbs of 5, 6, 7 and even 9 centimeters will not flower.

Some gardeners are likely to be impressed by extremely large bulbs. True, these look impressive on the counter, but those over 15 centimeters are likely to be discarded mother bulbs that will split the first year after planting.

Anything from 11 to 14 centimeters should be satisfactory.

Insects and diseases

About the only insect that is active at the time tulips appear is the aphid. These do no direct damage and are easily killed by a number of sprays available through seed stores. The only real damage they do is to infect tulips with the viruses that cause "breaking," and this only if they have previously fed on infected cucumber vines.

Tulip fire is serious where it occurs. I have never had it attack my tulips, but I have known cases where it ruined the flowers year after year. As already stated, it is a fungus disease (a Botrytis), which is picked up by the young shoots as they break through decaying organic matter. The fungus makes the petals look scorched. By keeping the ground surface clean and using only clean mulching materials over the bulbs, it can be almost completely avoided. If trouble does show up, fungicides available to control it are Captan, Fermate, Manzate, Phygon XL and Bordeaux Mixture. These should be applied at the first sign of trouble. If the disease was prevalent the year before, spray as the shoots break through the ground.

chapter four

Daffodils, narcissi and jonquils

The names applied to flowers that grow from bulbs treated in this chapter are highly confusing. They are misused so often that some explanation is needed before the beginner can tell what he is talking about.

They all belong to the genus *Narcissus* and for this reason when speaking of them as a whole it is proper to call them narcissi. Correctly, only the long-trumpet narcissi are called daffodils, but to many this, not narcissus, is the all-over name. To qualify as a true daffodil, however, a flower must have a trumpet as long or longer than the diameter of the six petals (called the perianth) surrounding it. These are often listed in catalogues as Trumpet Narcissi.

Next comes a group with trumpets from one third to slightly more than one third the diameter of the petals. These are the *Incomparabilis* class in catalogues.

Third are varieties bred from the wild sorts brought into cultivation by the famous collector, Peter Barr, and called Barrii. In these, the trumpet is stubby, less than one third the diameter of the petals. They have bright orange or red-orange cups.

Fourth are the Leedsii varieties with very short trumpets or cups, either white or very pale lemon yellow.

Fifth are the true jonquils, which are seldom found in commerce. This name is misused to designated trumpet narcissi more often than their right one. True jonquils are rather weedy little plants with round, rushlike leaves and flowers borne in loose clusters. These are not very impressive in appearance, and are of interest only for large collections, or possibly for naturalizing.

Sixth are the Poet's Narcissi, with very short, stiff cups and flat waxy petals. The cup is always bright in color.

Seventh are the small-flowered species, usually found in the wild and not too far removed from their ancestral type. The Triandrus hybrids, although usually classified elsewhere, are not enough different to justify this fine distinction in the amateur's garden.

Last (and not even least in the North) are the *Narcissus tazetta* varieties. These make considerable growth in the fall, and cannot survive prolonged freezing. Hence they belong in Florida, south Georgia and along the seacoast in South Carolina. These are the most intensely fragrant of all narcissi.

Hybrids between this class and the Poet's Narcissus do not inherit the fall-growing habits of the one parent, but do retain the characteristic fragrance. They are reliably hardy in the North. Although not often listed in catalogues, these *Narcissus poetaz* are highly desirable. They combine the intense fragrance and bunch-flowering habits of the *N. tazetta* type with the sturdiness and clear color of *N. poeticus*.

Color range

Unfortunately, the color range found in narcissi is less than will be found in a single class of tulips, such as the Single

Earlies. For this reason, they lack interest for the beginner who finds some of the subdivisions in the various classes too much like splitting hairs.

Colors include pure whites, pure yellows, white-and-yellow combinations, white with orange or reddish orange cups and yellows with orange or reddish orange cups. There are so-called pinks, but except under rather unusual weather conditions, these always seem to turn out shades of dirty buff or orange-salmon, nothing like the pink colors shown in some catalogues. I doubt that any of the pinks, with the possible exception of Mrs. Backhouse or Lovenest, is worth consideration by the beginner.

All this will sound like rank heresy to the real fancier, to whom some of the color nuances in the genus compare favorably with the flashes of color found in the diamond. At the same time, until the beginner has grown and enjoyed half a dozen or so of the cheaper sorts, he has no business paying the high prices which many of the choicer narcissi bring. With price tags as high as $150 for a single bulb, this is not a hobby for everyone.

In borders and beds

The high cost of the fancier varieties is all the harder to justify when we realize that all narcissi, from the tiny wild species to the giant trumpets are not suited for use in formal beds, but belong in less formal plantings.

The smaller species and their hybrids, including the Triandrus type are at their best in the natural setting of the rock garden. They are naturally at home here, since in the wild they are usually found growing among rocks or in stony fields.

The following should interest the beginner: Thalia, Agnes Harvey, the Hoop-Petticoat Narcissus, February Gold, Moonshine, and *Narcissus triandrus.*

Large trumpet narcissi that are reasonable include King Alfred, Beersheba, Golden Harvest, Mrs. Backhouse, Lovenest and Aerolite.

Among the *Incomparabilis* varieties I like the following low-priced ones: Francisca Drake, John Evelyn, Dick Wellbrand, Carlton.

Unless you are interested in a complete list, perhaps the Barrii varieties can be omitted entirely, although Diana Kasner, Fire-tail and Bath's Flame are good.

Perhaps the Leedsii ought to be included for cutting, for which purpose they are beautiful: representative varieties include Hera, Daisy Shaffer, Silver Star and Tunis.

As already stated, the true jonquils belong only in large collections.

The Poet's Narcissus belongs in every garden, if only for its associations. It flowers the latest of any narcissus. The bulbs are long-lived without having to be dug and reset. Ornatus Maximus is excellent, although Actaea is larger. The original type, *Narcissus poeticus ornatus*, the Pheasant's Eye, is a living antique that belongs everywhere.

For naturalizing

The most important place the narcissus fills, however, is not in the border, but in naturalized plantings. Nothing is lovelier in spring than a wooded plot carpeted with the gold of thousands of narcissi in full bloom.

For this purpose, unless cost is no factor, the best bulbs to use are those sold in mixture for naturalizing. The cost per bulb is low, and large areas can be covered at not too high a cost.

Such mixtures are a variable quality. Some dealers look upon them as a means of cleaning out surpluses. This can be good or it can be bad. If the surpluses are of high-priced varieties in small lots, some lovely things often show up. I once salvaged the gorgeous white variety Beersheba from such a mixture, at a time when it was selling for $2.00 a bulb.

I don't like to see the big trumpets naturalized. They look out of place when seen close at hand, although off in the distance they make a bright spot of color. If you buy a mixture off a counter, insist on picking out only the small bulbs that sift to the bottom of the bin. The dealer will be surprised (and may even give you a better price) because he is used to having customers grab only the largest bulbs. These large bulbs are practically always big trumpets.

If only one variety is to be planted for uniform effect, by all means, make it one of the *N. poeticus* varieties. They are far more durable and flower for a longer period of time without dividing.

One important point to keep in mind when naturalizing is that the plants should look natural. Don't plant in straight, regular lines, but rather in long "drifts" or islands among the trees. A good way to distribute the bulbs is to toss them out in small basket-full lots, planting them where they fall. Always throw them along in the same general direction. Make them look as though the colonies deeper in the woods or meadow had been blown there by the wind.

Because naturalizing mixtures contain all types as a rule, it sometimes pays to sieve the bulbs and sort them by size. By planting all the smaller bulbs together with the larger ones elsewhere, a more uniform effect will be gained.

Planting

Because of the many different species that went into the breeding of the modern narcissus, the bulbs will vary greatly in size. Some of the wild species will not be much bigger than an acorn, while double-nosed bulbs of King Alfred often weigh over a pound apiece. This creates a problem, since different-sized bulbs should be set at different depths.

A rule of thumb which works well is to plant them with twice as much dirt over them as the depth of the bulb itself. In loose loamy soil, they can go in a trifle deeper. This will mean about 1 to 3 inches of soil over the small species, while the big trumpets may be as much as 6 or 7 inches down.

Narcissi particularly resent being "hung" in a hole with an air space under them. A dibble is a poor tool for planting. For planting naturalizing bulbs, I prefer a stout grub hoe or mattock, which will penetrate to a good depth with a single swing. If the hole is too deep, a little of the clod it brings up can be crumbled to bring it up to level.

In the border, a good stiff trowel or a narrow tiling spade does a fine job.

Time to plant

Narcissi are not nearly so fussy as tulips about being planted late. They can be dug when ripe and reset almost immediately in shaded woods where soil temperatures remain cool. However, like tulips, they prefer cool soil, so if they are lifted in spring in warm sections, they can be stored in a cellar until fall. Much nonsense has been written about getting them in earlier than tulips. True, they cannot be kept as late on open shelves, but if the bulbs are kept in a 50- to 55-degree temperature, planting as late as December is entirely successful.

The only reason for planting them in September is that they will stand such treatment, which gets them out of the way before the tulips need attention. If bargains in narcissus bulbs can be had in December, and if they stand the cutting test (explained in the chapter on tulips) by all means buy them.

Fertilizers

In fairly rich soils such as are found in woods where leaf mold has accumulated, very little food will be needed for two or three years. Feeding the bulbs heavily merely steps up the speed with which they will increase and advances the day when they must be lifted and replanted.

Everyone who naturalizes narcissi sets out with a firm resolve to divide them regularly, until he tries to lift a few colonies and separate them from the tangled tree roots. He soon gives up, after which the bulbs are left to shift for themselves.

By using fertilizer with a light hand until the colonies are quite large, one can delay the need for division of the old bulbs. The time they really need food is after most people have given up and left them to shift for themselves—when each bulb is surrounded by half a dozen or more of its offspring. Then two tablespoonfuls of a good chemical fertilizer applied to each colony just as the shoots are breaking through the ground in early spring will do the trick. It will have no effect on bloom the year it is applied, but the next year should show results. Regular feeding from then on will pay.

Narcissi in lawns

I doubt seriously that the city man with a good lawn should ever try this trick. For it to succeed, the bulbs must be left growing until late spring, by which time the lawn has made several inches of growth. If mowed sooner, the bulbs will last for about two years before dying out.

Since it is impractical to lift bulbs naturalized in grass and heel them in to ripen off elsewhere, only such areas as can be left unmowed until late spring are suited for this type of planting. Mixed narcissi are particularly beautiful in orchards in sod.

Another fact to consider is that, when first mowing a lawn where the grass has been allowed to grow several weeks later than normal, other problems arise. Sometimes, because the clumps of bulbs cause a change in level, the mower will scalp the lawn, leaving an ugly bare spot. Again, because the grass falls over and mats down, an ordinary reel-type mower will not cut well. A sickle-bar mower is the best type for this job.

chapter five

Hyacinths

Omar was right when he recommended selling that extra loaf of bread and buying hyacinths to feed the soul. I am certain that he meant to imply that the path to the soul was through the nose. Surely there is no more heavenly odor on all this earth than that of hyacinths on a damp warmish spring evening.

As garden plants, hyacinths are not perfect. If they lacked fragrance, few would bother to plant them, since in form they leave much to be desired. They are satisfactory as pure color, except for one or two poor shades. The whites are virginal pure, the lavenders lovely and delicate, the purples regally rich and the pinks brilliant and clear. I have no use for the so-called yellows, which are actually of a greasy-ivory shade that is anything but attractive. The reds are harsh and strident.

In the right colors, hyacinths make magnificent formal beds, but are quite expensive if any sizable area is to be planted. However, for this purpose, the smaller 14- to 15-centimeter bulbs should be used, not the costly mammoth size used for forcing.

My favorite way of using hyacinths is as clumps of small

color accents in the perennial border. If grown in front of a group of irises, hyacinth spikes seem to be coming from the same leaves. Such clumps should be placed toward the front of the border, where their rich fragrance can be sniffed and enjoyed.

Culture

This is no flower for the offhand, careless gardener. While it is not difficult to grow, it is much fussier than most of the spring-flowering bulbs. It likes to be set at just the right depth in soil that is not too heavy, yet not too sandy. It must have good drainage, yet resents drying out.

In the right soil, a loose, mellow loam, it belongs about 4 inches below the surface. You can try it 3 inches down in heavy clay, and if the winter is not one that sees severe changes from warm to extremely cold, it will do all right. In lighter, sandy loams 5 inches down is about right, but extra watering plus extra feeding will be needed.

Like tulips, if fed too much, hyacinths will produce offsets and the old bulb will stop flowering. However, they are somewhat less sensitive in this respect, and in sandy loams definitely need a little extra food. In most moderately good garden soils, where other plants occupy the ground after the bulb season, no additional fertilizer should be given. The bulbs are quite sensitive to rot in rich soils.

Hyacinths are also more tolerant of heat and will flower well in the Gulf States if left in the year around. However, they are somewhat less resistant to cold and do not survive well much north of a line drawn from New York to Chicago. This range can be extended north somewhat by planting near a basement wall, so that heat radiated from the heating plant into the soils can raise soil readings higher than normally found at such latitude.

chapter six

The minor bulbs

I wish a better name than "minor bulbs" could be found for these. True, they are small in size, and are used less frequently than any of the bulbs considered so far.

Against this, when they are used, they are usually planted in rather large masses and the effects are anything but minor. One of the most thrilling sights in the plant world is a vast sea of millions of true English bluebells, *Scilla nutans,* flowering in the dappled shade of an open forest. There is nothing closer to pure poetry in all gardening. To call such a display minor is to belittle a noble species.

Time and time again, I have seen gardeners start out with a few grape hyacinths, without much idea of why they were planting them. After these have spread in regal splendor across several yards of shaded ground to form a sheet of lavender-blue, these gardeners come to realize that "minor" bulbs can produce a major effect.

Early bloom

The major role of these small bulbs is to provide bloom long before any other garden flowers appear. Many of them open their first buds while snow still lingers in the shadows during warm spells late in winter.

When this early-flowering habit is taken advantage of in the garden, the season is advanced at least a full month over that possible when narcissi are the first blossoms to appear.

Because they flower so early, minor bulbs are perfect for small open spaces that enjoy sun for only a brief time in spring. Where dense shade is cast by maples, which leaf out among the earliest of the deciduous trees, few plants can complete their life cycle soon enough to use this hour-in-the-sun. Here, the Winter Aconite, *Eranthis hyemalis,* often lives up to its common name of New Year's Gift.

Best of the minor bulbs

CHIONODOXA (Glory of the Snow): Although these come from around the Mediterranean Sea, they are perfectly hardy over the United States. This is perhaps the most vividly blue flower of its season, which makes it a perfect foil for the saucer magnolia, flowering almond and, where the strongly contrasting colors can be tolerated, for the forsythia. This gold-and-blue combination needs to be at a distance to be enjoyed; otherwise it is a bit startling.

For more delicate contrasts, there is a lovely soft lavender chionodoxa, and a clear pink and a white. The latter are not always easy to find, but are to be had.

Chionodoxa does well planted 3 inches deep in rather gritty soil with good drainage. For a year or two after planting, it is not very impressive. When it finally becomes established, it overruns large areas and forms sheets of bloom about the time crocuses are in flower.

SPRING FLOWERING CROCUSES: These are the most commonly planted of the minor bulbs. They are at their best just after the snowdrops and before the earliest daffodils open. The crocus is a favorite for naturalizing in lawns. For this purpose it is much more satisfactory than the narcissus, since it flowers and is almost (but not quite) out of the way by the time the lawn should normally be mowed.

This may be heresy, but any spring-flowering crocus that is not yellow is of little interest to me. The blue, white and striped varieties are interesting enough grown as pot plants, but to my taste, a crocus out of doors ought to be a bright buttery yellow.

The bulbs should be planted 2 inches below the surface. This is an adaptable species, however. If you make a mistake in the depth of planting, somehow the bulbs manage to pull themselves up or down to the right level. If the tops are left until they die down completely, in a soil that is not too heavy or too sandy, they will increase rapidly in grass.

Do not limit them to the lawn, however. They also belong in the perennial border, out in front where they can be seen. Because the bulbs lurk so close to the surface, they can be a nuisance in a cultivated border. I solve this by planting them among trailing stems of Baltic ivy or *Phlox subulata,* which protects them while they are dormant.

In natural rock gardens clumps of crocuses are highly attractive.

WINTER ACONITE (*Eranthis hyemalis*): About all that needs to be said about this golden gem (other than what has been mentioned) is that it resents being left on the counter of a seed store, where it dries out rapidly. This should be one of the first of the bulbs to be planted in fall. If left out too long, it can be seriously hurt and may not survive. It likes to be set an inch or two below the surface in well-drained soil. This is a good plant to scatter under the overhanging branches of shrubs. The foliage remains attractive a long time after the flowers are gone.

FRITILLARIA: In this group there are three choice spring-flowering bulbs. The most striking of these is the Crown Imperial, which is better seen than smelled. Some find the odor offensive. It does have a faint skunklike odor, but if not sniffed too closely, this is not bad. Children never seem to mind it and will go right up to the flowers to observe the bright honeylike nectar that forms in clear drops without falling.

This is a spectacular plant. The two-foot-tall spikes are topped with whorls of orange, terra-cotta or dull purplish flowers that really do resemble crowns. They have conspicuous contrasting veins. This species belongs in the back of the perennial border so its odor will not be too noticeable.

It also makes splendid clumps in open woods where it will form large colonies if it is happy. Quite often it multiplies so rapidly that these colonies should be divided every two or three years. It likes a woodsy soil with plenty of old organic matter in it. If growing where tree roots rob the soil of fertility, it will appreciate a feeding with a good mixed fertilizer when the flower spikes are breaking through the soil. In the perennial border, it needs no extra feeding if the other plants are fertilized during the summer.

The bulbs of Crown Imperial are soft and fleshy and dry out

rapidly when out of the ground. They should be planted as soon as the bulbs are available from Holland, usually in early September. Plant them about 4 inches deep.

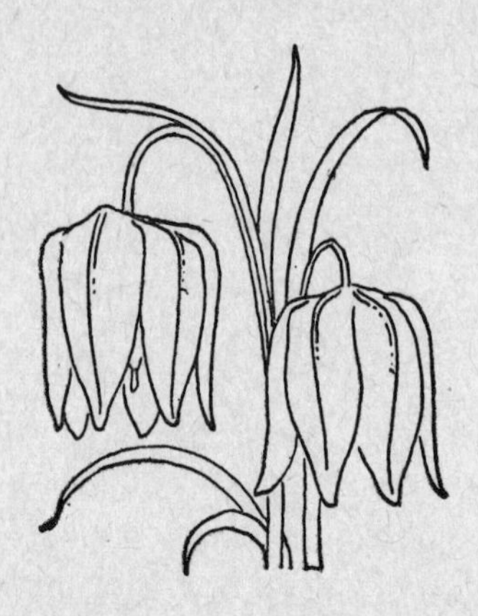

The Guinea Hen Flower from Europe, *Fritillaria meleagris,* is not for the formal border, but belongs at the edge of woods or under shrubs, where it can be fairly dry in summer. The flowers are marked with curious checkered patterns in various colors. One of its common names, Snakehead Lily, is suggestive of the reptilelike mottling found in these flowers. I find them more odd than beautiful, but they do have a charm of their own.

The Guinea Hen Flower should be planted 3 inches down. If in a location to its liking, it increases freely.

The third fritillary worth considering by the beginner is the Mission Bell from California. It is hardy about as far north as the New York-Chicago line. The flowers are striking in color—orange-scarlet nodding bells that brighten up partially shaded woods. They like woodsy soil with some leaf mold in it. Except on the West Coast, they multipy slowly.

GRAPE HYACINTHS (*Muscari*): If space is at a premium, minor bulbs might well be limited to crocuses and grape hyacinths. Easy to grow and multiplying with ease, the latter are so common that some professional horticulturists scorn them. They do not realize that to the beginner, this is a new and truly beautiful group of plants. I am constantly being amazed at the number of people who do not know this little gem.

Individually, the six-inch-high spikes are far from impressive, unless examined closely. Their common name is descriptive, the flowers resembling bunches of purplish grapes atop stiff stems.

There are a number of different kinds in cultivation. The one most frequently found in old gardens is *Muscari botryoides,* the starch hyacinth. However, modern catalogues have dropped this in favor of *M. armeniacum* which produces larger flowers and more of them. There is an improved variety of this called Early Giant, of a clear, light slate blue. This flowers ten days earlier than its parent.

A sweet little thing is the white grape hyacinth. The flowers look as though they had been cut from white wax. Some call this the pearl hyacinth.

An odd muscari that flowers much later than the others is *M. plumosum,* the feather hyacinth. It has for flowers attractively cut feathery plumes of a bright violet-purple.

All kinds of muscari should be planted about 3 inches deep. They are not too particular as to soil, but like a spot where the bulbs will be shaded during the summer months after the foliage dies down. They seed freely and will form vast sheets of bloom if allowed to grow undisturbed.

STAR OF BETHLEHEM (*Ornithogalum umbellatum*): This is also called Summer Snowflake and Sleepy Dick. Here is an interesting old-time bulb, often found growing wild where it has escaped from cultivation. Whenever an old garden is abandoned, one of the last flowers to succumb is the Star of Bethlehem. It is so aggressive, in fact, that it can easily become a nuisance unless surplus plants are ruthlessly uprooted and discarded.

This is definitely a plant for the wild garden, where it will form tremendous colonies. Plant the bulbs 2 inches down in any soil.

The starlike flowers borne on 36-inch stems have striking black centers. *Ornithogalum nutans,* a somewhat shorter flower than the above, is also called Star of Bethlehem and is similar in habit and growth.

A curious Ornithogalum for the South and for California is the Milk Lily, *O. arabicum.* It is much larger and more beautiful than either of the above, but so tender it can be grown out of doors only along the Gulf of Mexico and in California. The Milk Lily is grown by the acre in South Africa for use as a cut flower. The spikes are packed in boxes without any moisture and shipped to England and the United States. On arrival they are placed in water and quickly resume their fresh appearance. They will last for weeks in water without wilting.

SPRING SNOWFLAKE (*Leucojum vernum*): This is not commonly planted. I am guessing that most people who plant this bulb thought they were getting the similarly named snowdrop, a different flower entirely. The snowflake is really a very desirable plant, but blooms somewhat later than the snowdrop, so has more competition for attention. The flowers resemble giant lily-of-the-valley bells, with a curious brown spot on the end of the petal. They are quite permanent when well established. Plant 4 inches down in any woodsy soil.

SNOWDROPS (*Galanthus*): Because they come so early, children love them above all other spring-flowering bulbs. In the deluxe days of big estates with tremendous bulb beds, these were often planted in among tulips, flowering as the latter were just breaking through the ground. The foliage of snowdrops remains in good condition for a long time, hence makes a good ground cover for other bulbs.

They do well everywhere except where they are too wet. Plant them 3 inches down. There are double forms, but these seem too clumsy and heavy to deserve the name Snowflake. I much prefer the singles, of which Elwes Giant variety is by far the best.

SCILLAS (Bluebells and Squills): The Siberian blue squill is the most commonly seen form of this easy-to-grow minor bulb. Flowering at the same time as the snowdrop, the two are often planted together, for an interesting blue-and-white effect. The common form grows about 4 inches tall, but my favorite variety is Spring Beauty, which is taller and flowers about a week later.

The bluebell of English poetry is *Scilla nutans,* which for some reason is not too easy to find in American catalogues. It is perfectly at home here and hardy everywhere. Perhaps one reason it is not more popular is that it flowers later, about the time tulips are in bloom. However, no other flower in its season can match the vivid blue of this one. The white form is also charming, but competes with other white flowers in its season. The pink is in the same class.

The Spanish bluebell, *Scilla hispanica* (which some catalogues list as *S. campanulata*) is even later. This comes in blue, white, pink and lavender, with 15-inch stems.

Scillas should be planted 3 inches deep. The Siberian squill is easier to handle out of the ground; the other forms have a soft bulb that spoils easily. Plant these as soon as they arrive.

chapter seven

Lilies

My rose-loving friends insist that the rose is the Queen of Flowers. If that is true, I contend, then the lily is King. Certainly the most stately, the most truly regal of all flowers are the lilies. (One species, *Lilium regale,* is actually called by a name denoting its royal qualities.) If there is any argument on this point, I would like to have the doubter stand with me in an open glade in the woods where a noble clump of the true *Lilium giganteum* is growing.

Here is an awesome sight—tremendous inch-thick stems with enormous leaves towering 10 to 12 feet into the air and crowned by foot-long pure white trumpets of marvelous substance.

Not that the beginner will ever start with *Lilium giganteum.* This is the Nobel Prize of horticulture. To be able to grow this to flowering is considered the mark of a master gardener. It is Nature's doctorate for consummate skill in horticulture.

There are many gardeners who will argue that no beginner has any business working with lilies: they are too difficult to grow. There are others, equally competent, who will argue that lilies are among the easiest of all flowers.

The truth is that both of them are right—part of the time. There are probably seventy-five or more species of lilies that should be grown only by the breeder, collector or specialist, and then only with the realization that they may fail. I have grown over eighty species, about forty-five of which could be kept alive only by extensive coddling and nursing. If I had started with only these, I might have easily rated all lilies as of no value to the beginner.

On the other side of the argument can be found the beginner who selects ten lilies from a regular catalogue. There are lists offered in American catalogues of lilies that are nearly foolproof. With reasonable care in soil selection and planting, no real skill is needed to grow them.

How lilies differ from other bulbs

The lily bulb, which is usually made up of scales (instead of layers as in the tulip and narcissus) is a different organ from most bulbs. It is not a device for storing food in a short growing season to last through a long dormant period. Instead, it is a winter resting organ, much like the crown of a perennial plant.

Because it does not need to accumulate large amounts of food over a short period of time, the lily is not as efficient as other bulbs as a storage organ. It needs more food than other bulbs to produce its leaves, stalks and flowers. In the past it has been a superstition that lilies cannot stand fertilizer. According to new work at the Bureau of Plant Industry at Beltsville, lilies seem to need substantial amounts of plant food to make their best growth.

The old superstition that mineral or chemical plant foods are bad for lilies has also been upset. The Beltsville work shows they are not only able to absorb food better from such fertilizers, but have less disease than when organic manures are used.

In season, lilies differ from spring-flowering bulbs. They begin to open in late spring, winding up when the last blooms are caught by early frosts.

As might be expected, lilies differ considerably in their cultural needs from spring-flowering bulbs.

Soils

Through all this discussion of spring bulbs, we have paid no attention to the finer points of soil condition. As long as the soil is not too rich, most bulbs do all right.

When we take up the growing of lilies, however, soils become critical. One English authority describes the perfect lily soil as one so full of humus that it is "frothy" and so loose in texture that an arm can be thrust in it up to the elbow.

This does sound fantastic, but it also gives some idea of what lilies prefer in the way of soil. If we change "frothy" to "spongy" and "elbow" to "wrist," we come up with specifications for an ideal lily soil that would suit almost any specialist. Few of us will attain this heavenly perfection, but we can strive for it.

While there are some magnificent lilies that will survive in far less luxury, there are none that will grow anywhere on any soil and produce truly beautiful blooms. The two or three species that seem to grow everywhere and survive in old gardens are the upright cups like *L. elegans*, things of little beauty.

Acid soils best

Although one or two of the European lilies seem to prefer lime soils, by and large the lily is a plant that must have an acid medium to do its best. It is to a considerable degree a native of pockets of woodsy soils on slopes or in forest openings. Here, leaf mold, tannin from tree bark, decaying vegetable debris and other organic matter accumulate and produce soils that range from quite acid to almost neutral.

If the perfect situation for lilies could be created, it would be an open glade in a wood, where moisture from above trickled down the slope, across the bulbs and out the drainage at the lower end. Around the base of the lilies would grow shallow-rooted low plants to shade their roots.

The soil would be on the acid side, but not so much so that blueberries and azaleas grow better than other plants that like less acid.

In such a situation, all lilies would grow, and all but one or two of the European species would really thrive. Such conditions would be ideal. I mention them only so that such elements of this ideal home as are possible in your garden can be worked on. Now let us discuss several lilies that need no such pampering.

Depth of planting

The bulbs of lilies differ in character, and in the depth at which they grow. Some form creeping underground root stocks that meander beneath the surface for several feet before showing above ground. Lilies of this class do well at a shallower depth than do those that produce upright stems, form small bulbs along the stem, and also produce roots above the bulbs as well as at the base.

The latter group, called "stem-rooting," obviously need much more space above the bulb than do others, so there will be room for the stem roots and the new bulbs. They should be planted at least 8 inches down. In very loose, loamy soils, 10 to 12 inches of soil over the bulb is not too much.

Others form upright stems but do not produce stem roots. Such lilies seem to be happy about 5 inches down.

Two exceptions to these rules are the Madonna lily and the

Nankeen lily. Incidentally, these are unusual in other respects, too. In late summer, they throw up a rosette of leaves from the bulbs without producing a stem. If buried too deep, this rosette cannot be formed and the bulb dies. For this reason, these two species should be planted not over 1½ inches deep. Most lilies have what are known as contractil roots. If planted too shallow, these will actually contract, pulling the bulb down to a more favorable depth.

Planting time

If possible, all lilies except the Madonna lily and its variety the Nankeen lily should be planted in fall as soon as they are available commercially.

If you are moving bulbs from one bed to another, the best time to move them is just after the flowers fade, even before the stalk dies down. This will sound like rank heresy to old-time lily growers, but evidence collected at the Bureau of Plant industry shows that such bulbs make new roots rapidly, and are much more certain to bloom the following year than are those planted after the stalk has completely disappeared.

Incidentally, in my own tests, when lilies are moved at this time, they often produce many small bulbs just under the ground, which increases the stock of that particular lily in a hurry.

A few American lily specialists have been willing to dig their bulbs early so that their customers can plant before the date that bulbs usually come on to retail counters. Unfortunately, this always means that the bulbs are one or two grades smaller than they would be if left in until later, so the grower sacrifices potential income. Since prices are based on size, the buyer who can persuade growers to dig early should be willing to pay a premium for this service.

However, bulbs from Japan always arrive late. By the time the foliage has died down and the stocks are dug, it is late October, which means late November or early December delivery in the United States. I am still in favor of fall planting even if it must be done under rigorous conditions found in the North.

Planting in frozen ground

The best way to handle this problem is to prepare the holes for planting in advance. The earth removed is stored in a warm basement until planting time, and the hole filled with straw or leaves. When the bulbs arrive, the filling is removed, the bulbs set in place on the bottom of the hole and the unfrozen dirt from the basement poured over them.

If not available until spring (and many dealers refuse to buck habit), then the earlier planting can be done, the better. Too many gardeners think of spring as the natural planting time, and just don't ask for lily bulbs until then. To take care of this trade, bulbs are often kept in cold storage. If temperatures are right, this is safe, but too many dealers use the wrong temperatures, which stimulate unnatural early growth. Sprouted bulbs do not usually flower the first year.

It is well to make the holes for spring-planted bulbs the fall before and fill them with straw or leaves as already described. One precaution is necessary when planting in predug holes of this kind. With frozen soil all around them and loose material in the hole itself, these become perfect sumps for collecting surface water that runs into them. For this reason, drainage should be good. The usual recommendation that sand be filled around the bulb for drainage is silly: unless the water has some place to *go,* the sand merely fills up with water and is worthless.

Bulb treatment

Certain disease organisms can be brought in on bulbs. Before planting, I always dust them with either Spergon, Captan or Arasan. These fungicides destroy surface spores that might otherwise cause rot or disease. The cost is very low. Simply shake the bulbs in a paper bag containing a little of the fungicide until the bulbs are covered with a thin coat. Then plant.

Easy-to-grow lilies

Here is a list of lilies for the beginner—they are not temperamental and should grow well in the perennial border. Since they can use more plant food than other bulbs, they will tolerate the same fertilizer applications used on the other perennials. All of these will grow in the soil suitable for a mixed border, provided the reaction is slightly acid for some of them.

The bulbs are usually better off if planted behind (to the north of) a healthy clump of peonies, phlox or other vigorous perennials. This will provide them with shade in midsummer and keep the soil cool.

If some clean mulch can be used over the clump, this will also help. I am assuming that the border is watered at regular intervals and that the soil does not get bone dry. No lilies thrive in dry soils.

MEADOW LILY (*Lilium canadense*): This is one native lily that is not at all fussy. I have seen it growing in swamps on muck soils, in open meadows on rather stiff clay loams and at the edge of woods in sandy loams if these have plenty of organic matter in them. It does not tolerate lime, but is one of the few lilies which does not seem to mind being planted out in the sun.

It should be planted about 6 inches deep.

MADONNA LILY (*Lilium candidum*): This is a living antique which has been cultivated for centuries. It is portrayed on old Greek vases, in old tapestries and prints. This is one lily that seems to prefer a soil with a little lime in it. Also, it does not like to be shaded, growing well in the open border, but does like a covering over its feet. Do not plant it deeper than 1½ inches below the surface.

It has one peculiarity which is responsible for its reputation for being difficult. Unlike most lilies, it is only dormant for a short period in early summer. The rest of the year it is in active growth and cannot be safely moved. Soon after flowering, the flower stalk dies and dries up and the basal leaves die off.

This is the only time during the year that the Madonna Lily can be safely transplanted. Unfortunately, most of the bulbs in commerce come from Southern France, and the length of time they are dormant is hardly long enough to permit them to be dug, graded, wrapped, shipped and delivered in this country. They usually arrive in September, when Madonna lilies have already made their basal rosettes in this country. For this reason, bulbs should be ordered as early as possible and rushed into the ground without delay.

American-grown bulbs are usually more expensive, but worth the difference.

When in flower, the Madonna lily is a lovely thing—clear, waxy, nearly flat stars strung along a stalk about 30 inches tall. In season, it combines perfectly with the delphinium, and is usually planted as a companion plant to that perennial. A lovely apricot hybrid of the above is the Nankeen lily (*Lilium testaceum*).

LILIUM FORMOSANUM (no accepted common name): Many dealers offer this as *Lilium philippinense formosanum*, but it has not been found in the Philippines, so the shorter name is both convenient and more accurate.

It is particularly desirable because it grows quickly from

seed. If started very early in a greenhouse, most of the seedlings will produce a single flower the same year. Seeds sown in the open garden will flower the second year.

Flowers are long white trumpets, shaded pinkish purple on the outside and greenish yellow in the throat. Pure white forms are offered in seed. This is an excellent way to grow large numbers of lilies for naturalizing or for cutting. Older plants may produce as many as ten buds.

The bulbs are stem rooting and should be planted about 8 inches deep.

HENRY'S LILY (*Lilium henryi*): This beautiful recurved or Turkscap lily is soft apricot yellow with self spots. From five to twenty flowers are produced on a single stalk. One objection to this lily is that the stalk is quite soft and, unless staked, will arch over and touch the ground. Its best use is as a cut flower.

It will tolerate some lime but prefers acid soil. It is stem rooting and should be planted 8 inches to 10 inches deep.

LEOPARD LILY (*Lilium pardilinum*): This is a magnificent recurved lily with intense orange or scarlet flowers spotted with purplish brown. It varies so much in the wild that a single colony will produce almost every shade between soft orange or dull red to near-maroon, all variously blotched with these colors, but all spotted.

It is not fussy and will grow in any good garden soil in full sun. It has a creeping rootstalk and should be planted about 4 to 5 inches deep. It is extremely promiscuous and produces seedlings freely. If anything, it is too vigorous when happy in a location, throwing out new shoots everywhere. A single bulb has been known to produce as many as one hundred stems in a six-year period.

Its one demand is for plenty of moisture. It grows in bogs, but always on a hummock or slight rise, so the bulb itself is never under water. It is perfect at the edge of a pool above the water line. Elsewhere, just so the soil does not dry out, it will thrive almost anywhere.

REGAL LILY (*Lilium regale*): This is one of the easiest of all lilies to grow, and can be propagated in quantity from seed. Its fragrance is a bit too heavy at times, a rich, magnolialike odor that can be overpowering in a small room. I have had single stems with as many as twenty-four flowers on them. The white trumpets are bright yellow at the throat, stained pink outside. Pure white forms are available, but expensive.

This is the most widely planted of all garden lilies. It is stem rooting and should be planted at least 8 inches down. Although not fussy as to soil, it has one defect—it starts growth so early in spring that the top of the new shoot is often killed by late freezes, which finishes the bloom for that year. If planted on the north side of low shrubs or where the soil is shaded until spring, it usually does not start growth as early. Deeper planting, down to 10 inches, will slow up its appearance and prevent this type of injury. It prefers to have the bulbs in shade but the stems in full sunlight.

SPECIOSUM LILY (*Lilium speciosum*): Although millions of this lily are grown all over the world, there are still thousands of people who ask whether the cut flowers are orchids. The individual blooms do look like orchids when made up into corsages, and some florists call this the Orchid lily.

The flowers are white, stained pink and dotted with carmine. Sometimes the pink stain is so deep the entire blossom looks red. The petals are recurved and appear on three-foot stems, five to fifteen on a stem.

The fragrance is delightful, not too heavy or cloying. It flowers in late summer at a time when there are few flowers in the garden, just ahead of the hardy chrysanthemums. It is stem rooting and should be planted about 8 inches deep.

AMERICAN TURKSCAP LILY (*Lilium superbum*): This

is an easy lily to grow, happy in any moist acid soil. It resembles the Meadow lily but is somewhat stronger growing. Otherwise it is practically the same except that it should be planted 6 inches deep. One point in its favor is its long season of bloom. Individual plants in a colony will flower at different periods, giving a season almost two months long at times. July is the best season for it.

SIBERIAN MARTAGON LILY (*Lilium tenuifolium*): This has some of the most vivid clear scarlet flowers imaginable. They are Turkscap in form and are entirely without spots. A clear apricot-yellow variety called Golden Gleam is also available.

Usually the wirelike stems grow 1½ feet tall, but vigorous specimens may grow to 3 feet. Not at all fussy, but the bulbs are short lived. They will last longer, incidentally, if not permitted to produce seed. Cut off the faded blossoms promptly. Many growers start seed every year and keep young plants coming along to fill in. The bulb is rather small and should be planted about 5 inches down.

EASTER LILY (*Lilium longiflorum*): This is no place to go into the main strains of these true Easter lilies that now exist. They are too familiar in form to need much description.

There is one strain, however, which deserves special mention —the Croft lily, which originated in the Pacific Northwest. This is a husky, strong-growing form of the Easter lily which seems to be hardier than the others.

A beautiful colony of this variety has survived on an estate in Glencoe, Illinois, for several years, increasing several times. I have known of other small plantings in the Chicago and New York areas, all apparently perfectly hardy. This is such a pure, chaste lily when growing in the open that news of its survival in the North should be welcomed by discriminating gardeners. In the South, all forms winter perfectly, and the Easter lily is an excellent garden flower.

All Easter lilies are stem rooting and should be planted 8 inches deep in good garden soil which has some lime in it.

Forced bulbs planted out

Usually the gardener's first contact with lilies is through a potted plant at Easter time. Such plants can be set out in the open garden after flowering. The ball of earth, knocked out of the pot, should be set so that its surface is 8 inches down. This allows the stem to form some stem roots, although the root buds from which they are formed have often been destroyed. Such plants will die down, but soon make new top growth, flowering again in fall.

They seldom survive the winter, and are of value only for that one precocious bloom in fall.

Lilies from seed

Seeds of *Lilium regale, L. tenuifolium* and *L. formosanum* are offered by several dealers. These particular species will grow easily if seed is sown as early as the soil can be worked, and the bed is kept shaded and moist. Seedlings should be allowed to grow for a year and should be transplanted into their permanent bed the following September.

Seeds make possible the planting of big beds of lilies, or naturalizing them in quantity in woodlands.

chapter eight

Irises

The irises are an annoying group to the horticulturist who wants to classify all plants into neat packages. Some of them are bulbs and should be considered under that heading. Others have fibrous roots with the rootstalk part almost impossible to find. These really should be treated more like perennials. Others grow from a rootstalk (called a rhizome) and call for a third kind of handling.

Irises that grow from bulbs

There are three different types of bulbous irises commonly sold, but the distinctions between them are technical and of no interest to the beginner. The first of these, the Dutch, is merely an earlier variety of the Spanish. Latest of all is the English.

All these are interesting in color and form, but the English have the largest flowers. If there is any choice, perhaps the English should be picked for a first trial of bulbous irises. The colors are truly beautiful—clear, bright shades of blue, yellow and white, all of which have a bright yellow "target" at the base of the petals.

In listing these as hardy, I am being accurate, but this does not mean they can be planted out and left to shift for themselves. If planted in the North late in fall, they start growing in spring and are safe. If, however, they are planted too early, they make strong top growth that same year and are badly injured by freezing. South of the Virginia-North Carolina line, they can be planted out early in fall. Although they make foliage, they will survive the winter.

Elsewhere they are best planted out two or three weeks before freezing weather is expected. Mulched heavily, they will make their growth in spring. This delays blooming somewhat, which is an advantage, since otherwise they will compete with more spectacular flowers.

The purpose of the mulch is twofold. In fall, it slows down the freezing of the bed and allows root growth to take place. In spring, it slows up thawing, so the tops will not make precocious growth. Remove this mulch when the buds on apple trees and flowering crabs are showing color.

The soil requirements are about the same as for tulips. They should be planted 5 inches down. They need somewhat more moisture than tulips and may need water in dry springs. Because the list of varieties offered is quite limited, no recommendations are being made.

In the South, the variety Wedgwood (a somewhat different iris) can be planted out of doors. It has a clear blue color that is most attractive.

Iris reticulata is a choice miniature bulbous iris that is hardy as far north as southern New England. It will survive even farther north with a heavy mulch. Its chief charm is its powerful violetlike fragrance. The individual blooms are rather small and the whole plant not much taller than a crocus. This is a lovely species for the rock garden. The color is an intense violet-blue. Plant 3 inches deep in well-drained soil.

Irises with fibrous roots

There are only two groups of these irises of interest to the beginner. They have a rhizome of a sort, but it is surrounded by masses of fibrous roots so that they act more like perennials.

The first of these is one of the most striking plants found in the garden—the exotic, almost unbelievable Japanese iris. The first glimpse of a planting of this iris usually leaves the beginner breathless. The flowers, huge saucers of flat petals 10 to 12 inches across, look almost too frail to be alive. No flower I know looks as regal as a big purple-and-gold specimen at its best. Certainly, if they had more substance and could be used for corsage flowers in their season, any orchid would be put to shame. The pale blue-lavenders are particularly lovely. The whites are ethereal in their purity.

The flowers may have either three or six petals. This is not as important as it sounds to the beginner. On reading a catalogue list, he is likely to pick only those with six petals, thinking they are more spectacular. He is disappointed to find that the largest flowers are often those with only three petals.

Varieties misnamed

Unfortunately, Japanese nurserymen have never hesitated to change tags. I have had 10 different plants to which an identical Japanese name has been attached, only to find that instead of 1 variety I had 8. Or from another source, I might order 10 different varieties only to find that when they flowered they were practically alike.

This is most unfortunate because many of the Japanese names

are poetic and beautiful. Translated, they become such delightful labels as Morning Mists, View from High Places, White Foam, Jewels and Flowers, White Waterfall, Sky Amidst the Cloud, or Dancing Tiger.

However, we are interested in flowers, not labels, so the best course is to buy them in mixture and separate out the colors that please us. If the collection of a specialist can be visited in flowering season, some of these can probably be compared with named varieties. If *his* names are correct, you too can have Dancing Tiger and its companions in your garden.

Cultural needs

Many have shied away from Japanese irises under the impression that they are swamp plants which must grow in water and will not do in the open border. Since space at the water's edge is not generally found in small gardens, this noble group of plants suffers from neglect. Because it is so generally omitted and is virtually unknown, here is an iris which will provide the beginner with the means to create a spectacular garden with which to astonish his neighbors.

True, the Japanese iris does need lots of moisture while making its growth. All it asks, however, is that the soil not be allowed to dry out from early spring until after the flowers have faded. This does not mean growing them in a swamp or bog. Their need for moisture can be met very simply by applying less than a bucket of water to each clump any day that rain does not fall. If a length of hose is left hooked up, it is an easy job to give the plants a drink either in the morning or evening.

This is not an iris for sandy soils that drain rapidly, nor will it grow on stiff clay that bakes hard in summer. This is one plant that really enjoys plenty of organic matter in the soil. When the plants are set out, a shovelful of old rotted compost, decayed manure or peat moss should be mixed in each hole. Similar organic matter used as a mulch during the winter and worked under in spring is also good.

During the growing period before the buds open, 2 heaping tablespoonsful of a good mineral fertilizer around each clump will improve the size of the flowers and allow the plant to store food for its winter rest.

The Japanese use fish meal on their prize blooms. For those who prefer to use an organic fertilizer, the modern fish-emulsion liquid products are excellent. These come closer to the quickly soluble minerals in action, since all their food elements are dissolved in water, and are readily available to the plant. These fish-emulsion fertilizers contain the minor or trace elements in soluble form, extracted from fish scraps and offal by soaking. I have found these excellent if used in moderation—2 or 3 times during the growing period.

Dry in winter

Once flowering is over, water should be withheld if possible. Bogs where water stands over the roots close to the crown in winter are not suitable for growing Japanese irises. They must be on dry land during their resting period. This does not mean bone dry, but the moisture content of the soil should be no higher than that found in the average perennial border. If rains do not fall, water just enough to keep the soil moist.

Planting time

Gardeners usually order Japanese irises on the same order form as the bearded types. Because they come from the same grower, why not have them all delivered at the same time and save postage? Seems like a good idea, except the Japanese irises don't agree. They have entirely different needs and cannot be transplanted at the same time. The bearded irises are dormant in early summer and can be moved best at that time. But the Japanese are still in bloom when digging of the bearded types begins.

When the dealer tries to fill orders for both types at once, the Japanese, not dormant at the time, are badly injured. If, in addition, they are shipped dry, always a good practice with the bearded types, they are further damaged and may rot. The proper time for planting Japanese iris is autumn, about the time other hardy perennials are set out. They should not be shipped dripping wet, but should be protected with damp moss against drying out. If received dry, soak them in a bucket of water overnight before planting.

From seed

The Japanese iris is readily grown from seed, which is available in seed stores. Sow as early in spring as the ground can be dug; keep the soil damp continuously and the seedlings will appear in a few weeks. As seedlings, they need more moisture than other perennials, but don't like bog conditions. Plant them where they are to grow in fall.

Siberian irises

Another group of irises almost unknown to American gardeners are the Siberian varieties. They are perhaps the most graceful of all—a field in bloom looks like a ballet chorus rehearsing on a green lawn. The thin, reedy flower stems appear in early summer among the tall grasslike leaves.

In every way the Siberians should be handled like the Japanese, except that they can tolerate a little more drying out, and are thus better fitted for the ordinary perennial border.

Varieties do not change much in this group: recently I checked a catalogue issued in 1924 and found practically every variety listed today. Emperor, a dark, violet blue that may grow as tall as 48 inches, is beautiful. Perry's Blue is identical except that its color is a clear, sky blue. Snow Queen, the finest white, is somewhat shorter. It has a brilliant yellow "target" at the base of the petal.

Bearded irises

This is the group that nine out of ten people have in mind when they talk about irises, and almost invariably they think about the tall bearded type, not the smaller varieties.

Here is a group of plants about which pages could be written without exhausting its possibilities. There are literally hundreds of subdivisions of the class, which are of interest largely to the collector. There are forms that flower soon after winter has passed, while others may be caught by early frosts in fall. In height they range from 3 inches to well over 5 feet.

Dwarf bearded irises

These are extremely early. All of the kinds that are of interest to the beginner can be grown in any soil that will grow grass or husky weeds, what is commonly known as a good garden soil. With a little extra nourishment they will even survive on poor sandy loams. But they always want to be well-drained and exposed to the full sun. They prefer a spot that is baked by the sun in midsummer. The one thing they cannot stand is wet feet. Unfortunately, many gardeners, on seeing the wild swamp iris in bloom, assume that all members of the family need the same treatment and water them freely. Moisture forces soft growth, which is attractive to the Iris borer and is not as winter-hardy as firmer growth.

Planting depth

One mistake made in the past was the result of a clever phrase thought up by some author and given wide circulation. He described the iris rhizome as "riding on the soil like a duck floats on water." Consequently, for years iris enthusiasts have merely covered the roots on the rhizome, leaving the fleshy part exposed on the surface.

The result has been that plants have not done as well as they might. Tests of this method, compared with covering the rhizome completely, show the latter to be superior. When the upper surface of the rhizome is exposed, growth is less vigorous and fewer offsets are produced. The dormant buds from which the offsets arise are apparently dried out and do not grow strongly after exposure to direct sunlight.

For this reason, the best way to plant is to make a shallow trench about ½ inch deeper than the rhizome is thick. Lay the rhizome on the bottom and fill the trench with soil. The fan of leaves will be exposed to the sun.

Planting time

Irises can be moved at any time of the year and will survive. This does not mean they should be moved at any old time, but if there is a reason for doing so, it can be done.

The vitality of the iris rhizome is amazing. In tests, I have hung them dry from the rafters of a shed for a year. The only moisture they received was from humidity in the air. In spite of this abuse, they managed to survive and grew after planting.

This is by no means an argument for abusing them in this way. Such treatment always sets them back two or three years. There is, however, one time when irises can be dug and transplanted without hurting them in the least. It even improves the bloom, if the old plants were crowded. The right time to move them is between two and four weeks after the last flower has faded.

At this point the plant has completed its life cycle much in the same way as a tulip, which dies down for the summer, fall and winter. True, this rest period is not as prolonged as that of the tulip, but represents a similar situation. It allows the wild iris to survive summer droughts that make the conservation of moisture vital to the plant. Most of the areas from which the parent stocks of modern bearded irises came are regions where no rain falls during the summer months.

The roots of irises are annual and die off soon after flowering. When the short summer rest is over, new roots are produced and the plant begins to grow again. In the South and in California, new leaves remain green all winter long. Many varieties which need this winter growth are tender in the North. Light feedings of mineral fertilizers can be given after new growth starts.

Varieties of dwarf bearded irises

These charming little plants are seldom seen, but if given the conditions already described, they are easy to grow. They range from 4 inches tall up to about 12 inches. They open their blooms soon after winter passes, and are usually the first plants other than bulbs to flower in the perennial border.

The dwarf *Iris atroviolacea,* which in good soil grows about 5 inches tall, belongs here. It has red-purple flowers that are the first to appear. They seem far too delicate and frail to grow in the mixed border, but the plants are surprisingly tough and will thrive and increase without special care.

Iris coerulea, similar but sky blue in color, is not quite as rapid an increaser. These two early dwarf irises belong in every garden.

There are many named varieties of the dwarf types, including snow white, purple, yellow, reddish violet and sky-blue colors. Some of these were the result of crosses between the dwarfs and the intermediate varieties, resulting in some attractive plants that flower at 10 to 12 inches. Because new sorts are being produced yearly, the variety lists change too rapidly to be worth repeating.

Intermediate irises

The dwarf wild irises just mentioned were crossed with the tall bearded type to produce an intermediate class. These are actually "intermediate" between the two in size of bloom, habit and season. Although first introduced over half a century ago, they never became really popular until the big-scale promotion of other iris types brought them into the limelight.

During the past fifteen to twenty years, they have been coming out at a rapid rate. Although most varietal lists change rapidly, there are four varieties I believe should be recommended. These are distinct because they not only bloom in spring, but quite often produce a good second crop of flowers in fall.

Autumn King, a blue-purple bicolor is about 30 inches tall in spring, but closer to 24 inches when it flowers in fall. This is characteristic of this group: the fall flower stalks are somewhat shorter. Autumn Queen is about 20 inches tall. It is pure white with the usual yellow throat of the bearded class. Eleanor Roosevelt is a deep rich velvety purple on 28-inch stems. It is perhaps the most reliable of the fall bloomers, some of which sulk if the summer has not been to their liking. Southland, a 28-inch yellow of good substance and large size is also good.

Tall bearded irises

Here is a class which would take several pages merely to list in variety. Many people still call it German iris, although the true German iris is represented in commerce by very few old-time varieties, now almost obsolete. Actually, the modern iris is such a polyglot jumble of so many species that tracing its origins is a waste of time.

It has only been within the past few years that many of the old-time varieties, some of which had been in commerce for centuries, have been dropped in favor of the newer products of the hybridizer's art. While this prevents the compilation of lists of varieties, it does work to the benefit of the beginner.

A new variety introduced for from $15.00 to $25.00 a rhizome can be increased so rapidly that five years may see its price down to 50¢. This in turn makes obsolete a long list of excellent varieties, which must be disposed of somehow. These usually land in "collections" put out by growers.

For this reason, the beginner who knows nothing about iris varieties can make a start with a first-class list by simply ordering the best iris collection his seedsman has to offer. It may not contain late novelties, but this by no means dooms him to planting poor varieties. Actually, many of the highly touted improvements mean nothing insofar as the garden value of an iris is concerned. In the collection the buyer might find a variety like Wabash, a gorgeous snow-white-and-hyacinth-blue ruffled beauty that for three years was voted the finest of all irises by members of the American Iris Society. It is still superior in garden value to dozens of newer varieties that sell for fancy prices. New color "breaks," not the quality of the flower, usually distinguish novelties.

Colors

This brings up the matter of iris colors. The range is quite extensive, from pure white to sooty black, lacking only clear spectrum reds and pure pinks. Breeders are getting closer and closer to a true pink that is neither salmon nor lavender toned. The perfect pink, with beautifully placed blooms, and without a bright beard to detract from the color, is yet to be produced.

Iris reds are really vermillions or oxblood. These are really beautiful, but the fire-engine red of the Oriental poppy is lacking.

Although I have tried to stay away from mentioning varieties, I must make an exception for one variety, the magnificent William Mohr. This variety will be in commerce a long, long time because of its unique beauty. The mammoth flowers are pale lavender, overlaid with a brilliant violet-purple netting unlike any other iris in general commerce. The effect when seen for the first time is both startling and beautiful. William Mohr belongs even on the beginner's list.

Dividing

All the bearded irises present a real problem in keeping them growing vigorously. Their rhizomes increase so rapidly that they are soon too crowded to bloom well. The growing point of each rhizome will produce two or more offsets. These in turn will produce two or more each. Thus the minimum increase is sixteen in four years' time.

As can be appreciated, such fecundity can only lead to crowding unless the rhizomes are dug and reset every third or fourth year. This lifting and dividing takes place two to four weeks after the last flower stalk has faded. The chains of rhizomes are cut up into single growing shoots. Four such divisions can be planted in a square foot. Many iris enthusiasts plan to lift one third of their plants every third year, so they will constantly have young plants coming along for a good show.

Pests

The only real pest of the iris is the Iris Borer. This is the grub of a moth which lays its eggs at the base of the leaves. Entomologists say that there is only one brood yearly, but if this is so, the eggs hatch over an unusually long period of time. Newly hatched larvae occur from early spring to flowering time.

Eggs are laid in late fall but don't hatch until spring. After hatching, the larvae bore into the leaf. Many gardeners are fooled because they find the point of entry 6 to 8 inches above ground and think larvae are hatched from eggs laid in spring on leaves over 6 inches high. They don't realize that the eggs are laid low but that the hole moves upward with the growing leaf.

If the base of the leaf is examined early in spring, the egg masses can be found and crushed. In spite of this, however, some eggs will escape and there will be borers. Spraying with D.D.T. every two weeks from the time the apple blossoms show color until the iris buds begin to open, will kill young borers before they can make trouble. In the fall, a Lindane spray, applied every ten days from the time the first hardy chrysanthemums bloom until the first hard freeze, will kill the females laying their eggs, but it will not be needed if the spring D.D.T. spraying has been well done.

Iris rot is not a disease, but a secondary effect of borer damage Clean up the borer and rot does not occur except on wet, poorly drained soils. If the variety is one worth keeping, cut away the rotted parts of the rhizome. Then drop it in a bucket of bichloride of mercury solution (1:1,000) for half an hour. Your druggist can supply the bichloride of mercury and tell you how to use it. It is a deadly poison: treat it with respect.

Hardy amaryllis

The so-called hardy amaryllis has two scientific names in common use, and you may find it listed in catalogues as either *Lycoris squamigera* or *Amaryllis halli*. By either name, it is interesting and desirable in the late-summer garden.

The mysterious way it appears and disappears is probably responsible for its common name of Magic lily. In early spring, the green leaves appear above ground for several weeks but die down without flowering. Nothing more is seen of the plants until late summer, when the straight flowering stems suddenly break through the surface and, before the gardener is aware of what has happened, are loaded with lavender-pink trumpets that look like lilies. A planting of this bulb several years old may have hundreds of stems and will be a striking feature of the early fall garden.

As mysteriously as they appeared, the stalks die down and the plant is seen no more until the following spring.

The proper time to plant this unusual bulb is in early summer, after the bulbs have died down to rest before flowering. During this time the roots are dormant, and the bulbs can be moved without setting back their growth. Sometimes dealers sell this in fall after the flowering period to meet the demand inspired by flowers that have just faded.

Unfortunately, the roots are not fully dormant, and bulbs planted at this season may sulk for a year before flowering. Early summer planting is much more satisfactory.

RINEHART'S GARDEN LIBRARY

(continued from front endpaper)

taken care to select bulbs which will insure a succession of bloom from the first crocus or snowdrop, through daffodils and narcissi, on to tulips